Prayers
for
New and
Expecting Moms

Prayers
for
New and
Expecting Moms

Michele Howe

JOSSEY-BASS
A Wiley Imprint
www.josseybass.com

Published by Jossey-Bass
A Wiley Imprint
989 Market Street, San Francisco, CA 94103-1741   www.josseybass.com

Jossey-Bass books and products are available through most bookstores. To contact Jossey-
Bass directly call our Customer Care Department within the U.S. at 800-956-7739, outside the U.S. at 317-572-3986, or fax 317-572-4002.

Jossey-Bass also publishes its books in a variety of electronic formats. Some content that
appears in print may not be available in electronic books.

Library of Congress Cataloging-in-Publication Data
Howe, Michele.
Prayers for new and expecting moms / Michele Howe.—1st ed.
p. cm.
Includes bibliographical references.
ISBN 0-7879-6772-6 (alk. paper)
1. Pregnant women—Prayer-books and devotions—English. 2.
Mothers—Prayer-books and devotions—English. 3. Christian
women—Prayer-books and devotions—English. I. Title.
BV4847.H675 2003
242'.6431—dc21   2003010725

FIRST EDITION
HB Printing   10 9 8 7 6 5 4 3 2 1

Contents

Part Five: Living Outside the Box and Loving It! 131

To my mother-in-law, Nancy,
and my three sisters-in-law, Ana, Lisa, and Teri,
devoted mothers every one

Acknowledgments

Motherhood began for me some eighteen years ago when, newly married, I found myself pregnant after only six weeks of marital bliss! I was stunned, overwhelmed, confused, and unsure of my ability to handle all the adjustments of married life and the demands of a surprise pregnancy. Although I had no confidence in my own skills, I had rich resources in my family and friends. Looking back, I was so very blessed by the goodwill and kind attentions of these terrific ladies. They cheered me on, consoled me when I was afraid, and listened to me as I shared my deepest concerns. Because of their care and faithful love, I made it. Within the next five years, three more children were added to our family. As I look back, I can see God's plan was perfect—not easy, but perfect for us.

As you read these stories of other women, you'll notice a common thread running through each one. Every woman comes to the same realization that I did: we can't make it without God's strong hand of provision each and every day. And that's a good thing to recognize, isn't it?

That said, this compilation of stories for new and expecting moms isn't simply a collection of feel-good tales.

Although some will make you feel the "ooh and aahs" surrounding the joys of motherhood, others may cause you to step back and contemplate. But through each one of these stories, you'll see how other moms learned to redirect their struggles to God, who alone has the resource to take the joys and sorrows of motherhood and transform them into something beautifully enduring.

I would like to thank, once again, Mark Kerr, editor of the Religion-in-Practice series at Jossey-Bass, and his fabulous team, including Andrea Flint, production editor; Sandy Siegle, marketing manager; and Paula Goldstein, director, creative services. It has been such a joy working with people who take seriously the task of crafting a book so to heart. They do it exceedingly well and their efforts transform my mediocre communication skills into a product that simply shines. Though all their names are not listed on the cover, they should be. Every book is a collaboration of many gifted individuals who catch the same vision as the author and put their finest efforts into making it a reality. Again, my most sincere thanks!

Prayers
for
New and
Expecting Moms

PART ONE

Life Transitions

Anticipation runs high when a baby is due. Whether it is the emotional exhilaration of preparing for a nursery, selecting names, or attending baby showers, women can feel the excitement of change surround them. Although most of the pre-baby work is fun, some adjustments are challenging and demanding. From coping with dramatic shifts in body image, making the choice between breast or bottle feeding, or considering modifications to work schedules, every woman will find herself facing significant life changes as the big day draws near. Perhaps one of the most valuable attributes to hone is that of flexibility, for life with baby will never be the same.

I

He or She?

*E*veryone at the office had been pestering Renee to find out the sex of her baby ever since her obstetrician informed her that the optional procedure was her call. At thirty-five years old, Renee had jokingly told her coworkers that she'd already waited a good number of her adult years just trying to get pregnant. Another four months she could handle. Still, Renee wondered if she shouldn't go ahead and just get it done regardless. Her physician had explained to Renee that she was at a higher risk now due to her first pregnancy coming after age thirty. When Renee explained that even if her unborn baby had physical problems she would still carry her child to term, her doctor relented. But her physician advised Renee that ultrasounds were helpful in detecting unseen potential problems that the delivery team could be made privy to and prepare for prior to the actual birth. After she discussed this information with her husband, Tim, they decided to go ahead and have the ultrasound. "Just don't tell us the sex of the baby," Renee implored.

On the afternoon of the ultrasound, Renee and Tim sat waiting nervously. Suddenly the import of what had seemed to be a simple enough decision loomed large before them both. Renee started wondering about how just knowing a problem existed, if it did, would forever change the final months of the pregnancy. How would she handle the knowledge that something was wrong? Could she relax and enjoy the remainder of this long-awaited pregnancy? How would she respond to others' questions and their proposed solutions to such an emotionally charged situation? Just when Renee was about to get up and leave the waiting room, her name was called. Tim took Renee's trembling hand and gripped it tight.

Answer me when I call, O God of my righteousness!
Thou hast relieved me in my distress;
Be gracious to me and hear my prayer.
—PSALM 4:1

Dear Lord, I am afraid. I am honestly frightened that I may not handle the news that I might be called upon to hear. Suddenly, I am worrying about all the "what-ifs" again. This entire pregnancy has been such a gift to me. You know the long years I waited to become a mother. And now, when that precious time draws so close, I am wasting my days and nights fretting about the unknown. I cannot even sleep at night so powerful are my worries. At times, I feel paralyzed by a grow-ing apprehension that something will go badly wrong with my baby's development. Lord, only you can see what the coming days will bring. You alone are able to hold this world, my world, securely in its place. Teach me to lay my fears and my fretting down at your feet. Give me the strength and the good sense to leave them there. Instruct my heart in wisdom and give me a generous outpouring of your grace. Let not uncertain happenings spoil these treasured months of carrying my unborn child. Give me a strong and robust faith, one that will gladly face down the enemies of my soul. Encourage my heart when weariness and doubts begin to plague my mind. Bring into my life others of like faith who will speak words of comfort and consolation when I need it most. Surround me with your protection and lift my smallish mind to see beyond potential troubles. Open my heart and soul to receive this blessing with all the joy you seek for me. Thank you for your faithfulness and your goodness. I am so grateful for your provision of love and mercy. My greatest desire is that I learn this lesson of faith so soundly that I might teach it to my own child when the day comes. A greater lesson I could not bestow on my dear child, heart of my heart. Prepare me to be the mother you have designed me to grow into—in your time and through your grace. Amen.

Life is not a performance. The most important battles are fought where no one sees them.
—JERRY WHITE IN *Making Peace with Reality*

Ball Baby

Pam wished she had had the forethought to bring a pair of earplugs with her to her sister's house. After an hour of listening to her nieces and nephews either screaming for attention or screaming in earnest, Pam felt nearly deaf. Patting her own still flat abdomen, Pam wasn't exactly thrilled with the idea of becoming a mom herself. Married only two short months, Pam never dreamed she would get pregnant so quickly. But she had. A quick stop at Jean's might help me gain some perspective, she had thought. If anyone can help me get a better perspective on impending motherhood, Jean can. At least that had been her hope. "But it's certainly not working out as I had planned," she lamented as her niece threw her brother's Tinker toy creation across the floor, thus eliciting more yells from said brother. Just as Pam was getting up, ready to snatch her purse for a quick exit, Jean reentered the room with a tall glass of lemonade, Pam's favorite. She sat back down, resigned.

"OK, Pam, let's grab a few minutes while it's quiet and catch up a bit."

Was she kidding? Pam looked around the room to see if her normally sane sister had lost her mind. With three rambunctious kids under age six running helter-skelter through the house, she wanted to talk? Amazing, Pam bristled. Taking a sip of lemonade, Pam looked up at Jean who seemed oblivious to her chaotic surroundings. Gulping down the rest of her drink, Pam abruptly looked at her watch, made her excuses and walked out fast. Outside, Pam dug around for her keys, "Where are they?" she said in frustration. "Must have left them inside." Re-entering Jean's kitchen, Pam looked around but found no keys. Just when her spirits couldn't sink any further, Pam's niece sidled up to her with an exuberant smile as she offered Pam her keys, now attached to a ribbon with a red construction paper heart hanging from it. "For you, Aunt Pam," and she held Pam close. Unexpectedly, Pam felt the first surge of expectant joy rush through her, and she began to feel hopeful.

Thus says God the Lord,
Who created the heavens and stretched them out,
Who spread out the earth and its offspring,
Who gives breath to the people on it,
And spirit to those who walk in it,
I am the Lord, I have called you in righteousness,
I will also hold you by the hand and watch over you.
—ISAIAH 42:5–6A

Dear Lord, each part of me is hard pressed to accept the truth of my condition. This shouldn't have happened to me—not yet. I'm just not ready to become a mother. It's only been a short while since I married. I'm still getting used to being a wife.

Everything has changed so quickly. Marriage, now mother-hood. I'm still reeling from the news and I can't seem to gain a foothold on this. How will I manage marriage, working, and being a mom? I'm not ready for more life changes. Lord, I understand that children are indeed blessings from your hand. I believe that you have a purpose and a plan for my life. Yet I never expected this! I had my life planned out pretty well, thank you. I didn't want children for some years. Lord, I can't do this alone. I'm so weary of trying to figure out how to make it all work. I've cried more tears in the last few weeks than in my entire life. And no one seems to understand what I'm going through. People offer celebratory congratulations while I struggle to make my whimpering response. Intercede for me, please. I need your strength and your perspective. Extend to me a good measure of grace and show your benevolent mercy toward me. I am weak, weak and unsure, frightened and overwrought. Lord, I cannot walk this road without you. Be my arm of strength to lean upon, my wisest counselor, and my dearest confidante. Amen.

No, parents, you are not paranoid. Babies really have been sent into your life to confuse all your plans, to frustrate your best intentions, to outwit you at every turn and to drive you to your knees. In short: to reduce you to tears, just like themselves.
—MIKE MASON IN *The Mystery of Children*

3
Weighty Matters

Jill closed one eye and squinted through the other as she tried to see what the scales read. Sixteen pounds already, Jill lamented. Checking the wall calendar, Jill counted the weeks since her baby's conception. Twelve weeks along and I've already gained over one third of the total weight the doctor recommended. As Jill began mentally tabulating her progress, she guessed she'd be way over her OB's recommended weight gain if she kept the pace she had set. Well, Jill thought ruefully, it will be nothing new. I've fought against the extra pounds my entire life anyway. But Jill's more realistic thoughts soon gave way to some inner panic.

She went into her kitchen and stood there trying to decide what to eat. Instead of focusing on eating a nutritious meal that both she and her baby needed, Jill was thinking in terms of low-calorie, low-fat, and low-carbohydrate. She didn't want to put back the weight she'd worked so diligently to take off just a few years earlier. Jill always expected to fight a battle against regaining her weight as the years wore on. But she never considered how difficult putting on the needed and expected healthy weight while pregnant would be to her psyche. She loathed going into her monthly exam and getting weighed in front of God and everybody. Jill cringed when the nurse announced her gain for everyone to hear. Then her physician would repeat her weight gain during the exam. It was as though the weight police were buffeting Jill from every angle. She didn't need to hear it. Jill was already trying to maintain a balanced and healthy attitude toward the changes occurring in her body. Still, Jill thought with determination, I've lost the extra pounds before and I'm sure that running after a little one will help me do it again.

> *But godliness actually is a means of great gain, when accompanied by contentment.*
> —1 TIMOTHY 6:6

Dear Lord, what have I gotten myself into? I am fighting against my own good health and against the changes taking place inside me. I don't think I can stand to see how much my body is going to alter these next months. This is so difficult for me, Lord. You know my past struggles with accepting my body and all my difficulties in learning to work with my metabolism and genetic disposition. I have been so diligent in eating right and exercising, and now all that for nothing? Will I be doomed to see all my efforts come to naught? Even though this weight gain is temporary, I'm afraid that I won't be able to take it off once my baby is born. If I'm really honest, I still want to diet while I'm pregnant. In fact, I'm fighting against that temptation even now. Lord, help me gain some much-needed perspective here. I must, first and foremost, care for the well-being of my unborn child. Show me how shortsighted it is to be more concerned about my body image than about life in general.

In my heart, I know what is true and right. Still, I struggle against what my body is doing. I'm realizing that this wondrous work is being wrought without any effort on my part. Certainly, I must continue to take care of myself, yet you are creating a life within me and it's as though my body has taken control of me! I know this sounds foolish, but it is overwhelming to my mind. I feel and experience all these new sensations taking place and it's almost as though I'm an outsider. Lord, help me relish these next weeks and months. Give me your precious perspective and teach me to appreciate this miracle within me. Lord, this isn't just about me anymore. Help me grow up and start thinking about this little one who will soon be with us. Continue to teach me that acceptance and contentment in the midst of change is a great gift in and of itself. Never cease to transform my often-misguided heart, Lord. I know my weaknesses well. Please be with me and refine me as you see fit. For your sake and the sake of our baby, I pray. Amen.

The burlap bag of worry. Cumbersome. Chunky. Unattractive. Scratchy. Hard to get a handle on. Irritating to carry and impossible to give away.
—MAX LUCADO IN *Traveling Light for Mothers*

4
Just Concerns

Megan was pregnant. But she wasn't excited, nor was she happily anticipating telling her husband, Kurt. Megan still winced in memory of the last time she became pregnant and the emotional aftermath that had followed. At thirty-three years old, Megan had conceived four times previously. Every one of those conceptions had ended in miscarriage. By the end of the third month, she lost each precious child. After each of her miscarriages, Megan grieved bitterly, vowing to never again put herself through such misery. "We'll adopt," Megan told Kurt. But Kurt disagreed. He had read too many "miracle" stories about women who had experienced unfortunate track records similar to Megan's yet had gone on to carry a child to term. Megan listened to Kurt quote the statistics, trying to turn dismal numbers around to make them appear more hopeful. Yet Megan resisted. She was the one whose body had to endure the horrible pain of miscarriage and the emotional strain that losing one's child places on a woman. So, for the time being, Megan and Kurt had called a truce: no more adoption planning from her and no more pep talks from him. They both realized the other needed some time to heal from their most recent loss.

Fast-forward five months: Megan is again pregnant, but this time she is under the care of a fertility specialist.

Unlike many of her fellow patients, Megan has no trouble getting pregnant. Still, her previous losses put her in a high-risk category. Megan is troubled when she hears the news, but a minute part of her dares to believe that this time, under these circumstances, she might be able to carry her baby the entire nine months. What Megan doesn't want is to hear the overly exuberant voice of Kurt, whose enthusiasm, so reminiscent of her four previous pregnancies, would resound in her heart only as bitter reminder of what they'd already lost. But suddenly realizing that she must not hang on to past disappointments, Megan stops herself short and sends up a plea to her loving Father to help her turn a corner in her emotions and begin to rejoice over this new life within her.

Surely our griefs He Himself bore,
And our sorrows He carried.
—ISAIAH 53:4A

Dear Lord, can I endure another tragic loss? I don't believe I am able to shoulder the burden of another miscarriage. I cannot go back to that place of grieving again. Lord, you will have to meet me right where I stand—now, even at this very moment. I do not want this burden upon me any longer. I am in a stranglehold of consuming fear and do not know how to free myself from it. Hold my heart, my soul, in your able hands. Regard me as one who is immeasurably weak and frail and unable to handle the strain of living with such sorrow. Lord, I need you as never before. I am helpless and stagnant without your steadying hand of strength. Bestow your grace upon me, I plead. Even my heart is unstable, conflicted, and filled with worrisome thoughts. Lead me to a place that is safe and secure.

Shelter me, Lord, from the torment and instruct my heart in your ways. Give me a new vision for life. Help me see past all the agonies of these losses and give me your grace to place them into your hands. Safe keep all my hopes and desires for a family, Lord. And temper these longings with the overarching desire to live the life you've planned for me with resolve and courage. Shoulder me up through these coming weeks and months with your precious promises of mercy and peace and the joy of your fellowship. Let me not drift from your love; keep me close, and minister to my broken heart. I know that you love me. I trust in your sovereign reign over all things. Yet I'll never understand the whys behind so many of my heart's questions. Beyond my unanswered pleas, Lord, lead me to a place that is higher than where I am now. Lead me home to you even as I walk in faith through this pregnancy. Amen.

The Word of God pierces down into the unseeable me to release the invisible God. It floods my uncertain way with life. . . . The Bible works deep down and its chief work is to remind us that Jesus loves us.
—CALVIN MILLER IN *Jesus Loves Me*

Options, Please

$\mathcal{M}$arie had a secret goal. No one else knew how much it meant to Marie, because she was afraid others would try to talk her out of it. Having had one cesarean birth, Marie was determined to have her next child naturally. When Marie said "naturally" she meant it. After listening intently to countless other women who birthed their babies with the help of a midwife and who took the principled approach that the body already knows what to do, women just need to let it work, Marie ached to go this route when her baby was due. Already seeing a midwife was putting Marie in good stead. She was mentally and physically preparing for her baby's upcoming birth. Marie and her midwife carefully went through the prospective birthing process and planned as much as anyone is able. Marie was assured that her chances of having a natural delivery were excellent. With the medical staff on the ready, Marie felt comforted that even if her own plans went awry, a doctor was ready to take over and perform another cesarean if need be.

Still, as confident as Marie felt personally, she didn't want to let it be known what her intentions were. She'd already heard enough of the doom-and-gloom tales of women who tried to avoid a repeat C-section. That she wanted to do it with no drugs was another rung up the ladder of impossibilities to many of her family and friends. Why would you not want to take advantage of the painkillers available? Are you certain your abdominal muscles won't burst when you start pushing? Marie could almost predict the dire predictions she'd be likely to hear. Listen she might, but then Marie would go home and talk the matter out with her spouse and her midwife, do some more research, and, above all, pray.

Give ear to my prayer, O God;
And do not hide Thyself from my supplication.
Give heed to me, and answer me;
I am restless in my complaint and am surely distracted.
—PSALM 55:1–2

Dear Lord, thank you for your attentiveness to my prayers of late. I am so grateful that I can know you are close by and listening to my petitions. Lord, I believe in my heart that this desire is given me from you. Otherwise, I would not have the courage to forge another course. Please help me maintain a sense of calm well-being as my preparations for delivery draw to a close. Demonstrate your strength to me as I lean heavily upon you for reassurance and encouragement. As I continue to plan, let my thoughts and mind be disciplined and orderly. Let me not give way to debilitating worries and fears. I am confident that you are in control of all that transpires within my life.

Help steady me under your watchful gaze of loving protection. Extend your arm of support to me even now. And please, I ask that you would protect me from those who might unwittingly bring anxiety with their careless comments. Keep a shutter upon the mouths of anyone who would bring doubt or discouragement to us. Lord, we are indeed in your hands. We look to you for wisdom and support. Let our trust in your provision not be in vain. Even now, I am tempted to doubt and to turn back to another more familiar path. But I believe you have something better for me if only I would have courage to try. Take this, my body, and use it to bring a new life into this world. I commit this, oh so miraculous event, into your care and keeping. Bless my feeble efforts and give me your good grace to see it through to its completion. Surround us with those who are both wise and skilled. Work through them to deliver this child. I thank you for your love, unbounded and unconditional toward me. I pray that I would always look to you for all that I require. Amen.

We let go of stress and restore peace when we take the attitude that only God is God. Only God is perfect, unfailing, ever-present, and never-leaving.
—DAVID HAZARD IN *Reducing Stress*

6

Late Notice

It was the Fourth of July and Sara's family was going to attend the fireworks downtown. At the last minute, Sara's husband poked his head back inside the door and issued one final invitation to join the rest of the family. "No," Sara rejoined, "I've already told you, I'm not going anywhere until this baby is born." "OK," he apologized, "we're leaving now." As Sara peeked out the window and watched them drive off, she felt overcome by emotions of despair and loneliness. Looking down at herself, Sara felt even worse. She was absolutely humongous, she was sore and achy, her stomach itched, her feet were bloated, and she wanted to have her baby—now. Sara couldn't describe how desperately she prayed her baby would arrive within the next twenty-four hours.

Already seven days overdue, her OB had casually remarked that Sara really wasn't "progressing" too much yet. Could be a week, he predicted. You're wrong, she had wanted to counter. You try carrying around an extra forty-plus pounds, and in this heat no less. Sara's usual even temper was lost these days. She was also troubled about a decision she had to make before her next weekly exam on Tuesday. Since she wasn't dilating and her cervix wasn't thinning, Sara's OB suggested inducing labor. As soon as he said the words, Sara's temper snapped. "What about my plans to go naturally? Isn't this interfering with my body's own timetable?" After a long and controversial conversation, Sara left the office with more information plus some added confusion. Although in theory she had totally been against any "outside" interference during her pregnancy and upcoming childbirth, Sara was losing her resolve. She was exhausted and anyone who suggested a way to get the baby on the road to delivery was a godsend in her book. Sara eased herself into the recliner, sipped her water, and decided not to think about it anymore. Today she was going to relish the quiet and relax.

Lead me in Thy truth and teach me;
For Thou art the God of my salvation;
For Thee I wait all the day.
—PSALM 25:5

Dear Lord, please undertake for me now. I am surrounded by information and opinions and advice from everyone, and I am drowning in the overflow. I realize that my loved ones only desire what is best for my baby and me, yet this constant questioning is making me ill. I can scarcely cope with getting through the day, let alone being harangued by the unstoppable quizzing on such private matters. Lord, I doubt if I will even have the stamina to make it to my own baby's delivery. My heart and soul are despairing because of my body's discomfort and weariness. I never expected this all-encompassing exhaustion to take such an emotional toll on me. I've always been strong, energetic, and resilient. These days, it is something grand if I can make it through my day without hourly rest breaks. As much as I am anticipating my baby's birth, I am longing even more for this pregnancy to be over. I want my body back. I need my body back!

Help me make it through these final days of pregnancy with good grace. I admit my temper has been short. I have snapped and snarled and been thoroughly disagreeable. Please forgive my irritability. Give me your strength hour by hour to complete the needed preparations. Bestow on me your hand of guidance and assist me as I decide what medical options to select. Clothe me with a humble heart and let me not be ashamed or discouraged if my plans must be altered. Let me concern myself only with doing what is best for my child. I ask you now, Lord, for a good night's rest. I pray my little one would sleep when I do. Let him get comfortable within my womb and settle into slumber so that I might be rejuvenated and ready for the hard work of delivery. Calm my heart and mind. Soothe my emotions and stay close to me. I need you as never before. I hunger for your gentle touch of comfort. In my most worrisome moments, I place my life and that of my child into your care and keeping. Amen.

Your biggest weakness is God's greatest opportunity. Instead of complaining and begging God to change your circumstances, why not ask Him to fill that void with His strength?
—CHARLES STANLEY IN *How to Handle Adversity*

7

Difficult Reminders

On her knee, Barb sat jostling her best friend's child. In her heart, Barb was petrified. Barb loved children, always had. She had a natural, unpretentious disposition that drew youngsters to her like a magnet. No matter where she was, Barb could spot a child and immediately find something in that young one to relate to. It was a gift; at least that was what her friends told her. Today, Barb didn't feel so blessed. It was the beginning of her now-weekly OB appointments. The last stretch in the race toward delivery. Although Barb was overcome with joy as she anticipated these final days of pregnancy, she had to fight the waves of fear that intermittently suffocated her heart. If only she could forget, Barb frequently told herself. Look ahead, not back, was her well-spoken watchword. Still, how could a woman forget the tragic circumstances surrounding her own mother's death? Such horrific memories don't fade with time.

Barb picked up the precious bundle, now asleep, and carefully handed her over to her friend. Speaking now in quieter tones, Barb agreed to spill it—all. Those closest to her had a right to know what she was battling against. During the next hour, Barb shared her mother's story. A young happily married woman gives birth to a baby girl.

Life is good, everyone is healthy, content. Then the mother becomes sick and after a lengthy illness, takes her own life in despair. Her five-year-old daughter is left behind with vague, shadowy memories of a mother who left her alone, too suddenly, too soon. Over the years, Barb would hear the sordid details from extended family members who clucked their tongues one time too many. She never really could understand how or why her mother decided to commit suicide. Even into adulthood, Barb continued to ask why. But the answers never came. Now, at the eleventh hour, Barb had chosen to take the step her own mother never had: she started sharing her heart, and as she did new hope surged through her body and soul.

And in the same way the Spirit also helps our weaknesses; for we do not know how to pray as we should, but the Spirit Himself intercedes for us with groanings too deep for words.
—ROMANS 8:26

Dear Lord, how can the mistakes of others hold us in such a vice-like grip? As an adult, why can I not forget the sadness that seeped into every portion of my childhood? I want to let go of the pain, the hurt, and the unanswered questions. I try to. Yet every time I believe I've turned a corner and found peace it eludes me again. Lord, I do not understand any of the reasons behind the pain we suffer in life. I don't have the answers to the questions I need to find. Will you guide me through this process of letting go? Set me free from the doubts that linger in my mind. Help me to push past the fears that threaten me when I am weakest.

I want to relish every moment of my pregnancy, but my heart is frail and my faith is shaky. I don't seem to know how to pray anymore. What exactly should I come into your presence in petition for? Emotional healing? Mental stability? Spiritual maturity? I am at a loss. Please undertake for me now. Cover me with the blanket of your love. Bestow on me your enduring peace. Wrap me tight with your gentle care. I have great need of your closeness now. I desire nothing more than to live a life free from worries and burdens of the past. Show me how to let go, set me free, I pray. Infuse me even now with your spirit of power, love, and soundness of mind. Demonstrate your strong provision to me in my state of dire neediness. I count upon you every hour, every minute. I put my future hope in you. Amen.

We want God to know the earnestness of our heart. We beat on the doors of heaven because we want to be heard on high. We agonize. We cry out. We shout. We pray with sobs and tears. Our prayers become the groanings of a struggling faith.
—RICHARD J. FOSTER IN *Prayer: Finding the Heart's True Home*

8

Body by Design

Judy decided to spend the remainder of her evening finishing up her book on breast-feeding. From everything she'd read, nursing a baby was so much more beneficial than bottle-feeding. Judy learned that a child's immune system was stronger, there was less chance of digestive problems, and it helped tighten the maternal bond between mother and child. The only aspect of breast-feeding Judy wasn't keen on was that, at least until she learned how to pump her own milk, her husband Craig could have no part in feeding their newborn. That and the obvious fact that she'd be the one up each night for some months. Still, Judy was sold on the idea of nursing. How long, she hadn't decided yet. Now if I could only get Craig on board with this, too, Judy reflected.

Before she could think of some way of convincing her loving spouse, Judy heard the voices of her in-laws. Leading his parents into the living room, Craig took one quick glance at the book Judy held in her hand and motioned for her to put it away. With a confused grimace, Judy tucked the book into the pile of parenting and baby care books on the table in front of her. My word, Judy thought. As they sat chatting about incidentals, Judy's mind continued to wander back to the spats she and Craig had already weathered on the subject of how to feed the baby. Judy was incredulous that any man as intelligent as her husband would take issue with breast-feeding. She really couldn't figure out where he got his bias against it. After all, wasn't a woman's body designed to not only birth her child but to nourish it as well? While Judy and her mother-in-law hadn't specifically discussed breast-feeding between themselves, after seeing how nervous Craig had become when he found Judy reading a book on breast-feeding and his parents' unexpected visit, Judy understood. It wasn't Craig who cared; it was his mother. Judy brightened as understanding dawned; she suddenly realized that perhaps with some gentle instruction and kind conversation, she might be able to shed some new light to her spouse and his family.

Let everyone be quick to hear, slow to speak and slow to anger;
for the anger of man does not achieve the righteousness of God.
—JAMES 1:19–20

Dear Lord, I thought I knew my spouse so well, yet I've just been hit square in the face with another revelation. I am amazed that even now after years of marriage that we continue to surprise one another. It is also unfathomable to me that my strong, secure spouse could be so affected by his family's views. Lord, I admit to struggling with this myself. I find people around me frequently taint my own ideas. In this situation, Lord, we are at an impasse. Will you intercede for us? Please help us listen to the other's thoughts and concerns

with open hearts and receptive minds. Let not any precon-
ceived notions take over our desire to truly hear each other's
arguments. And show us how to speak in a way that evidences
our mutual respect and care for one another. I pray that we
learn how to work through delicate issues with unconditional
love and the highest level of commitment. Keep the views and
opinions of others, even family, far from our debates. Teach us
to listen and consider wise counsel, then come together as the
unique and separate family unit we are to make our own
choices.

As we struggle to find our way, let us each be confident
in your constant presence and ready willingness to buoy us up
during difficult moments. Give us your wisdom and knowledge in all matters. Help us not underestimate the feelings
and opinions of the other. Above all, temper our tempers
with your gentleness and grace. Let your words of affirmation
and understanding become the watchword on our lips. Lord,
I commit this situation into your capable hands. I trust in
your timing to set things aright. Be with us now, continue to
do your marvelous work of transformation in us both. Amen.

Feelings are important. First of all, they were created by God,
and anything molded by his hands has intrinsic worth.
—CAROLYN AND CRAIG WILLIFORD IN Faith Tango

9

Sanctuary

*I*n her hands, Olivia held her grandmother's ragged leather Bible. It was worn and crumbling around the edges. No matter, Olivia treasured countless endearing memories of her grandmother reading to her when she was just a child. Olivia closed her eyes and felt the aged leather, all creased and scarred. She could almost hear her grandmother's voice mingled with her own as she read portions of scripture aloud. It was always the same. Olivia would dash in the door after school, toss her books, and run to the kitchen for a snack. Her grandma never disappointed her on that point. Olivia could imagine the wonderful juicy raisin-filled sugar cookies and the ice-cold milk that was served up on those early fall and late spring days. During the cold winter months, it was hot cocoa and buttered toast. Olivia never tired of the standard fare; she somehow relished the continuity as much as the snack itself. As Olivia filled her tummy, her grandmother filled her soul. Reading as Olivia ate, Grandma always had just the right stories picked out for that particular afternoon. How she knew what to share on any given day remained a mystery to Olivia. But the truth had a way of seeping deep within Olivia's childish heart, and there it stayed.

Gone many years now, Olivia's grandmother had given her treasured Bible as a remembrance and as a challenge.

"Read this every day, pray for those you love, expect great things from God," she had said in her no-nonsense fashion. This was the message Olivia replayed. And so now she was carrying on in her grandmother's stead. Seven months pregnant, Olivia was already praying for her unborn child. Olivia spent some quiet time each evening with Grandma's Bible, searching its pages for insight, encouragement, and wisdom. She prayed thoroughly and completely for God's hand to surround her child and use this dear one to make a difference for all eternity. The more fervently Olivia prayed the more she resembled her grandmother's faithful and tenacious spirit, and Olivia smiled at the thought.

Make me know Thy ways, O Lord;
Teach me Thy paths.
—PSALM 25:4

Dear Lord, good evening, Lord. I'm back again with an eager heart and a willing spirit. Open my mind to glean all the good things you have for me this day. Let my thoughts be focused and clear. Help me set aside the busyness of the day and forget for a time all that still needs to be accomplished. Hold my attention and keep my mind from wandering, I pray. I sit here in expectancy awaiting your presence and your truth to unfold before me. Guide me as I read and meditate upon your word of hope, encouragement, and instruction. Lead me to pray for those whose needs are so great. I ask that you would lift the burdens from the weary and give instead a draught of healing refreshment to those in pain. Lord, protect your dear ones in whatever state they find themselves.

As I sit before your throne, I ask that you would continue to work within my heart. I am discovering how fickle my faith truly is. Help me set down a firm foundation so that I will not be tossed here and there by every wind that blows across my path. I hunger for a faith that is rock solid and secure. Will you brush away anything that would cause me to stumble and doubt? I feel compelled to pray for my own spiritual state as I contemplate becoming a mother soon. Truly, I am not prepared to face such a task on my own. I know all too well my own shortcomings. But I also believe you will make up for my lack. I count on this! Lord, continue to work within my heart. Let your ongoing process of sanctification never cease. Let me embrace the uncertain with a sure hope of your ever-present precious spirit, which leads me, guides me, and directs my every step. Amen.

When the babies came and it got more difficult to find time to read, I made a rule. I didn't have to open my Bible if I didn't want to, but I wasn't allowed any "me" time until I had read it. No sewing, no television, no chatting on the phone. The Bible came first.
—JEANNIE ST. JOHN TAYLOR IN *How to Be a Praying Mom*

10

Double Duty

With her tummy extending out, Trudy felt hard-pressed all around, literally. She tried moving from one angle to the next, but each time she sat down to nurse her eleven-month-old son, it was tricky. As Luke squirmed while he nursed, Trudy simultaneously felt the baby kick. "Ouch, that smarted." Looking up, Luke smiled. I'd better be quiet myself or this is going to take all day. Trudy realized how distracted babies got whenever they heard a noise or saw something move at this age, but all of this off and on stuff was getting to her. Maybe it's because my body is trying to do two different nurturing acts at once, she surmised. I know my friends think I'm crazy to continue nursing while I'm pregnant. And I do see their point. But Luke only nurses in the morning and at bedtime now. I really do want to make it through the first year of his life. I know it sounds silly to some mothers, but everything I've read tells me how much benefit Luke is getting from my nursing him his entire first twelve months. And, Trudy realized with relief, we're almost there.

How could I have guessed that I'd get pregnant while nursing? I knew there was a risk, but it had taken over four years to conceive Luke, so I never gave it a thought. So I'm on tandem duty for a while. It won't be forever. I just have to ignore those doomsayers who tell me I'm jeopardizing my health. Haven't I gotten the go-head from my OB? When another twinge interrupted Trudy's thoughts, she realized she was mentally counting down the days until Luke's first birthday arrived. Two reasons to celebrate, she thought happily!

If any man has ears to hear, let him hear. And He was saying to them, "Take care what you listen to."
—MARK 4:23–24A

Dear Lord, I am in awe once again at the way you've orchestrated the timing in my children's conceptions. What a surprise it was for me to discover I was pregnant, and so soon after the first. Lord, I'm not upset, I'm truly thankful for the blessing of another baby. Yet I admit to having been take unawares by this. I'm finding that I'm not so flexible as I once thought. This new development has me scrambling to alter my well-laid plans and make the appropriate adjustments. I am also finding myself second-guessing my past choices and wondering if you are thwarting them or fulfilling them. You alone see the future and all it holds, so I must continue to trust that your way is best.

Lord, you know my heart's desires in all things. Will you give me a sensitive spirit that hears rightly your voice when you speak? Even now, I believe I am making a prudent choice, but others beg to differ. Am I mistaken? To whom should I listen? Will you intercede for me even now? Give me a wise and intuitive heart that truly hears the message you intend for me. Let me not give way to fear or to the worrisome meddling of those who do not understand the situation. Lead me to an understanding of your will for me, not only in this circumstance but in all areas. Do not let me stand confounded by myriad voices, but let me tune into your words alone. Lord, I pray that you would protect my children; surround them with your blanket of care. Give soundness and strength to their bodies and minds. Envelop them in your mighty arms, and let me rest in the knowledge of your sovereignty. I am so thankful that you are always close by and ready to intercede on my behalf. I am astounded by your unconditional love and your generous provision. Always at the ready, you are my lord, leader, and wisest counselor. To you, I ask for all that I require, both in wisdom and understanding, for this day. Amen.

Relating to Jesus isn't a one way street, but a thoroughfare of travel in both directions.
—MARK D. ROBERTS IN *Jesus Revealed*

11
Stay-at-Home Mom

*C*hristina had looked at the clock once, twice, three times within the last thirty minutes. She could hardly wait for her husband, Jim, to arrive home from a weeklong business trip. Christina made a last inspection around the house. Liking what she saw, she felt pleased, sort of. With the housework done, the laundry folded and put away, ironing complete, and dinner at the ready, Christina should have been satisfied. Instead, she was filled with an underlying nagging sense of incompleteness. At eight and one-half months pregnant, Christina seemed to be getting what other moms warned her about: the nesting instinct. But they were wrong. Christina wasn't nesting, she was fleeing—at least in her mind. "If this is what I'm experiencing," Christina muttered, "then I need to jump out of the nest."

Troubled by doubts about quitting her full-time job as a realtor, Christina kept wondering whether she'd made the right decision. I've worked so hard to get where I am today, she reflected. Am I making a mistake? Two months ago, it sure didn't seem like it. What with Jim traveling so much, I'd be the primary caregiver for our baby anyway. We didn't want to entrust our newborn to just anyone, so here I am. Awaiting the big day and not doing a very good job at the waiting, I'm afraid. Every day that passes brings new

and different causes for concern. Will I make the adjustment from full-time career woman to stay-at-home mom?
I thought I could, but now I'm wondering. Is it too late to
change my mind? What would Jim think? We've already
spent more hours debating this than I care to remember.
Maybe it's just the hormones doing a number on my psyche. At least for the next eight weeks, I'll be here to stay,
after that who knows?

*I will instruct you and teach you in the way which you
should go;*
I will counsel you with My eye upon you.
—PSALM 32:8

*Dear Lord, I am unsettled. I cannot remember a time when
I've been so unsure of a choice as important as this one, Lord.
I truly believed that we had come to a definite and final decision. Now, after having had a trial run, I'm not sure I'm fit to
stay at home twenty-four/seven. I realize all this trepidation
may fall away once our baby is born. Perhaps I'll feel nothing
but gratitude for the indefinite adjustment time here at home.
But then again, maybe not. Lord, will you still my fears? I'm
finding myself getting all worked up about something that I
cannot change at now in any case. I am committed to my family above all else, but if I start to feel unsettled and anxious to
be out and about, will I cause my child harm with my divided
affections? This, too, troubles me. I wish I knew that without a*

doubt I could fulfill all my obligations without any regret. Naïve, aren't I? I suppose if I am very honest, I want the best of both worlds. I don't want to have to choose. Oh, Lord, whenever will I learn that life doesn't afford us all that we desire? Help me be content right where I am now. Let me learn how to live today. I experience nothing but discontent and frustration when I try to second-guess what tomorrow will bring. Ease my anxious heart and place your calming spirit deep within my soul. Prepare me to enter into the hard work of motherhood with a positive and joyful attitude. Let not selfishness or laziness hinder the good I can accomplish within the confines of my home. For the time being, I am here to stay. The coming months are still a mystery to me. Yet I am fully confident that as the days and weeks unfold, you will make the way clear to us. Lord, I commit my future into your hands. Continue your abiding work within my heart. I am yours always. Amen.

> *He knows all about you, inside and out, past, present, and future. And He recognizes the subtle symptoms of emptiness . . . symptoms such as dissatisfaction.*
> —ANNE GRAHAM LOTZ IN *Just Give Me Jesus*

PART TWO

The Littlest Big Adjustments

M otherhood is a long, singularly unique experience that demands the very best of a woman. When sleepless nights run together, after weeks of illness make the rounds through the family, during sparse financial stretches, moms need perspective—an eternal perspective, to be precise. Physical exhaustion may take its toll, disagreements on parenting styles may ensue, but eventually, most mothers find themselves tearfully wondering whether they're up to task of motherhood. With a temporary respite or a miniretreat from the routines and a lot of prayer, every mom can recharge and be ready with a response of love in answer to every demanding request. It's what mothers do best!

12

New Moves

*J*ulia and husband Dave had been married twelve years and in that time had moved six times, cross-country no less. As a computer software designer, Dave's field was ever changing. Since both of them loved a new challenge, frequent relocations weren't an issue. When the company Dave was currently working for started having financial problems, Dave contacted his recruiter and the job search began. Julia, at the same time, discovered she was pregnant. Together and with great expectations, they embraced the thought of becoming parents. Within weeks of her baby's conception, however, Julia became ill, and instead of adding the pounds, she was losing them. During one of the worst waves of Julia's sickness, Dave was out of town for a second interview with a potential employer—situated, again, across the country.

For the first time, Julia discovered she didn't like Dave being gone and the thought of moving sent her emotions through the roof. It was too much, Julia cried to herself. I could handle the moves, enjoy them even, when it was just the two of us, but now we need to settle down and establish roots somewhere. And then there are our families, too, Julia realized. I'm going to want them close and I need them to be part of this pregnancy.

When Dave arrived home the following evening, he had good news for Julia, or so he thought. "I got the job, it'll be a promotion in fact," and he beamed. Julia made cursory congratulatory remarks and then promptly burst into tears. "What is it?" Dave asked with concern. "We need to talk," Julia responded. "And maybe make a plan to stay put for good."

For just as the sufferings of Christ are ours in abundance, so also our comfort is abundant through Christ.
—*2 Corinthians 1:5*

Dear Lord, I am reminded of the psalm in which David cried out to you and lamented that his bed was wet with his tears, so earnest were his cries. I feel the same way. I am unable to stop the weeping that is erupting from somewhere so deep within my heart that even I am amazed. Lord, where is this coming from? Never before have I felt so unable to handle the changes my life demands. I feel paralyzed. It is as though my heart and mind are saying, enough, no more pressure. Lord, I am afraid that I will continue to cling to my fears past a point of no return. Undertake for my well-being, Lord, I beg you. I am so very aware of my weakness. Indeed, even my once strong body has not ceased to remind me of how frail I truly am. Everything that I once took for granted is now suspect. I am wondering how I'll manage and whether I'll regain my strength in time to cope with what's expected of me.

I'm ashamed to admit that I haven't thought about how my actions of late have affected those I love. Please forgive me. I know that I am causing pain to my family as well. Help me see past my obvious limitations. Give me your abundant grace to press past this time of trial. Show me clearly that you will not abandon me to my own worst fears. I realize that I have not been calling on you for my provision. I've been attempting to work things out on my own again. Perhaps this present struggle is to teach me to look to you in both good times and difficult ones. Let me see your face, Lord. Shine your love into my soul and allow me even a brief glimpse of your holiness! I am without hope if I depend upon my resources alone. I know this to be true. Forgive me for allowing self-pity to rule in my heart of late. Change and transform the way I think. Remake me. For your sake and for the sake of those I love, let me look to the future with great faith and high expectations. Amen.

Attitude is that "single string" that keeps me going or cripples my progress. It alone fuels my fire or assaults my hope. When my attitudes are right, there's no barrier too high, no valley too deep, no dream too extreme, no challenge too great for me.
—CHARLES R. SWINDOLL IN *Strengthening Your Grip*

13

Desperation Detour

The spare bedroom door slammed shut and Nina heard the lock fasten tight along with her heart. "This is so unfair," she cried. "Who ever said that parenting was a shared activity? I always thought we were in this together." Realizing that there was no help from her harried spouse any more that night, Nina paused, listening for her daughter's cries. Silence. Wouldn't you know it, she lamented, once we get into an argument to beat all, the baby finally settles in to sleep. Still upset from the perceived injustice of having to do the majority of nighttime care-taking, Nina decided a cup of herbal tea might calm her enough to eventually fall back to sleep.

As she prepared her drink, Nina recalled Jeff's words from earlier in the week when he came home to find her crying over something trivial. What was it he had muttered as he headed to the bedroom to change, something about having always believed that nothing could be worse than Nina's monthly PMS and now this? "Well, he's right, PMS was bad—but I'm living proof that post-baby emotional swings are even worse," she stammered through her tears. What's so sad is that everyone told me how wonderful it would be to have a baby and that we'd be living on sheer joy for months. That tired cliché certainly hasn't been the case for us. With the baby colicky and up so much at night,

I'm so exhausted I can't even summon up the energy to pin-point what my feelings are anymore. Then when I ask for help, especially at night, Jeff reluctantly gets up to rock her. Even then, I'm still up several more times every night. They tell me this will pass, but right now I need more than a ten-uous promise to cling to.

So that you may walk in a manner worthy of the Lord, to please Him in all respects, bearing fruit in every good work and increasing in the knowledge of God; strengthened with all power, according to His glorious might, for the attaining of all steadfastness and patience.
—Colossians 1:10–11

Dear Lord, it is remarkable to me that I, who once so stal-wartly believed that nothing would ever come between my spouse and me, have allowed our own child's needs to do so. I am so grieved that I have neglected our relationship during a time when we ought to be rejoicing in the new birth of our baby. Knowing that I have caused pain and heartache to one dearest to me hurts more than I can say. Lord, I understand this is a time of real adjustment and change. Yet I have not been willing to exercise any self-control when it comes to having my needs met. This is not good. Help me learn to communicate my desires and expectations in a way that is honoring to you. Show me how to ask for help in the right manner and not allow my exhaustion to turn me into an angry and bitter woman.

Lord, family is so precious. And I thank for you for this wondrous blessing. Please teach us both how to be godly parents. And let these lessons begin with our attitudes and actions toward one another. Let not impatience, irritability, fatigue, or weariness become wedges between us. Help us both understand the needs of the other and work hard to meet those needs cheerfully. Engage our hearts with your purpose. Give us a vision for parenting and family worth that spurs us on to greater deeds and higher commitment. Change us from within, Lord. Begin even this moment a new and fresh work within our hearts, souls, and spirits. Let our love for each other be a witness of your great love for all mankind. Guide and protect our family, Lord. We count upon your generous measure of grace and strength to see us through. Never, ever let us give in to discouragement or a spirit of despondency. Bring a revival of long-lasting commitment and love to our hearts and home. Take our shaky introduction to parenthood and build a strong foundation of faith upon it. Amen.

This is revival—the constant peace of God ruling in our hearts because we are full to overflowing ourselves, and sharing it with others. People imagine that dying to self makes one miserable. But it is just the opposite.
—ROY HESSION IN *The Calvary Road*

14

Body Wars

Under duress, Kate went shopping for a bathing suit. Normally, Kate loved clothes shopping but at eight weeks post-baby, Kate wasn't ready to examine herself beneath the unflattering lights in dressing rooms. But she didn't have any choice. With a family vacation on the calendar, Kate needed a suit. Like every other new mom, Kate had assumed that shedding baby weight would be a breeze. Hadn't she eaten well all during her pregnancy? And wasn't she up and about every morning taking her usual three-mile walk? Still, although the scale didn't register much additional poundage, Kate grimaced upon close inspection after showering. Stretch marks made silvery paths across her abdomen, her once flat muscles now sagged from the pulling, and one of her thighs showed the tiniest beginnings of a varicose vein—all in part due to her pregnancy and the extra strain those thirty pounds had placed upon her body.

Kate sighed. Determined to bring herself back into top physical condition before her upcoming vacation, Kate almost felt as though her body had betrayed her. Could she ever look the same the way she had before she became pregnant? Kate wasn't sure, but she was certainly going to make the attempt. Plotting out her ambitious workout schedule on her daily calendar, Kate sighed again as the baby started to

45

cry. After a quick diaper change and a feeding, Kate settled into the rocking chair and held her son. A few minutes quickly passed. Before Kate realized it, almost an hour disappeared as she continued to gaze at her son's sleeping form. I don't know what I'm so uptight about, Kate scolded herself, my body may not look like it once did, but if a few stretch marks and some sagging are the price of entering motherhood, I've no complaints.

For all that is in the world, the lust of the flesh and the lust of the eyes and the boastful pride of life, is not from the Father, but is from the world.
—1 JOHN 2:16

Dear Lord, I'm surprising myself again. I'm finally waking up to the fact that my life is not my own. I suppose becoming a mother has brought this truth home to me more clearly. Perhaps I always harbored the misconception, and a grave misconception it was, that once I fulfilled my maternal duties for the day, I would be free again. But this is not so. It is ironic that my own body confirms this. No matter the day or the time, I am constantly reminded by the changes in my own physical form that I have started on a new journey—motherhood. And this path will ever weave in and out of my days no matter how grown my child is.

Lord, this may seem so trite a matter, yet I sometimes long to have the pre-mom me back again. As much as I adore my child, I still feel a loss of sorts. There is a part of me that is gone forever. Could it be that I'm just nurturing that discontent humans often experience? That desire for something we cannot ever lay claim to again? I'm not sure. Yet I do know that I need and must live my life fully now. I cannot allow small sacrifices to spoil the joys of motherhood. Truly, before me I see such possibilities, and I am eager to bring all my resources to bear upon creating a loving home for my family. Yet my heart is also torn at certain moments. I still admit to some silent grieving over what has been. Lord, help me understand that all of life demands choices, and with those decisions comes the inevitably of having to set aside other desires. I am just beginning to walk this journey as a mom. Will you stay by my side and guide me? Entreat my heart to continue to give my best each and every day. And enable me to press ahead with no regrets and no sorry excuses trailing in my wake. Amen.

So many things we achieve are achieved only through struggle and conflict, not in easy ways. They always seem to involve crosses. I have so longed to find somewhere in life, some corner where joy is unmingled with pain. But I have never found it.
—JOHN GOLDINGAY IN *Walk On*

15

The Most Precious Commodity

Stuffing the pillow over her head, Beth tried to drown out the cries of her son. Tossing and turning—it was no use, Beth could never sleep when she knew her child was still up and fretting. "Do what the doctor said," Beth could mentally hear her husband's plaintive voice right before he drifted off to slumberland. "Right," Beth mumbled to herself. The pediatrician had said it was normal for youngsters to start waking up again even months after they learned to sleep through the night, but she didn't explain to Beth how wretched she would feel listening to her child "cry it out." With one backward glance at her husband's prone form, Beth was tempted to toss her pillow at him as she left their bed. I'll never get any sleep this way, Beth complained. I need sleep, I want sleep, and I have to have a full night's rest!

With her robe wrapped tight, Beth crept into the kitchen to get a glass of water. Then she silently padded her way to her son's bedroom door and listened again. It was quiet. But it won't last, Beth considered. I'll just wait in the living room for a few more minutes and make sure before I get back into bed. Glancing at the hall clock, Beth noticed it was 2:30 A.M. already. Well, if I can get back to sleep right away, that gives me another four hours before I have to get up again. If only tomorrow wasn't so busy, I could just possibly grab a few more minutes of rest. Closing her eyes, Beth still fought the urge to go back to her own bed. There was nothing she hated more than climbing under the comforter and settling into her cozy spot in the bed, just to be awakened mere minutes later. So Beth waited, eyes heavy, head nodding off, until all was quiet. The next thing she knew, she was awakened by her own cold feet and an achy back. "Must have fallen asleep," Beth murmured, "what time is it now? 3:55 A.M.? So much for getting another four hours of uninterrupted sleep in the morning. But when baby naps at 1:00 P.M., I'll be slumbering, too."

And after you have suffered for a little while, the God of all grace, who called you to His eternal glory in Christ, will Himself perfect, confirm, strengthen and establish you.
—1 PETER 5:10

Dear Lord, I never imagined I could feel so weary. There is a tiredness that seeps into the deepest part of my being. My body is achy and sore. My mind is sluggish and slack. Even my spirit is worn thin. I wonder how much longer I can go on with so little sleep. Day after day, I try to balance my responsibilities with getting the rest I require. But it seems that I'm thwarted time and again. There is so much to do and so little time for me to accomplish it all. Before I had a child I was able to spring into action early in the day and work until I completed my tasks. Now I barely have the strength to make out the to-do list. I'm out of steam, Lord. And I'm plodding through my days with little enthusiasm. Please do something to shake me out of my stupor.

I am thinking it is more than simple exhaustion. I believe I'm fighting half-heartedly against complacency. It's almost as though I've given up. I've resigned myself to believing I'll never live a normal life again. Forever I'll be constrained to living this lonely, nocturnal existence. Lord, give me clarity of mind and a renewed vision for life. Help me see past these temporal hardships. Give me your strength to meet the day's challenges with a positive outlook and a firm faith. Show me how to best order my days and bestow upon me your goodness and joy. Come near to me. Reveal yourself to my narrow mind and let me understand how great a God you are. Renew my spirit with yours. Let me rediscover the joy of mothering and the joy of living. Amen.

When God holds out hope, when God makes promises, when God says, "It can be done," there are no exceptions. With each new dawn there is delivered to your door a fresh, new package called "today."
—CHARLES R. SWINDOLL IN *Improving Your Serve*

16

Decisions, Decisions

I t was Saturday evening and Peggy sat rocking her sniffling one-year-old son before bedtime. The worst of this change-of-season cold was over. But little Jared still sported a red nose and a lingering cough. Peggy was grateful that Jared's cold hadn't developed into a secondary infection like the last time. He was definitely on the upturn health-wise. In fact, earlier in the day he was toddling all around the house playing with and chasing their family dog. Soon Peggy would have to decide whether or not to take him into the church nursery again. Peggy was due to teach another Sunday school class in the morning. Her husband was out of town, and that left Peggy with few options. Either she stayed home and cancelled the class, for it was doubtful they could find a replacement at this late hour. Or Peggy would take Jared to the nursery and leave him while she taught. Either scenario was a no-win one.

Peggy still shuddered about being told by the nursery director not to bring sick children into class the last time Jared was recovering from a cold. But then a few moments later, a matronly volunteer had practically whisked Jared from her arms, telling her that she'd watch him and not to worry, there weren't any other children using the nursery that morning anyway. Hence Peggy's dilemma. She had read the rules about using the nursery, and it was clear: no child with a fever, vomiting, or any contagious illness was allowed past the gate. Yet many of the volunteers understood that coughs sometimes lingered for several weeks, even after the virus has taken its course. What to do? It was times like these that Peggy wished she could beg off and let someone else decide. She realized it was no major decision; still, she wanted to do the right thing by everyone, so she sat down with deliberation and asked God for good sense.

But the goal of our instruction is love from a pure heart and a good conscience and a sincere faith.
—1 TIMOTHY 1:5

Dear Lord, I'm so grateful that you are always available to listen to my prayers and cries for help. I understand that this is no urgent matter that I'm bringing to you now. Yet I'm unsure of the right choice to make. No longer is it just my life I must consider. I am now responsible to make decisions that will be best for my child as well as his age mates and their families. It feels silly coming to you and asking you to help me determine what is the best course to follow. But I know you are concerned with every area of my life, even the smallest and most inconsequential. Be my guide now, Lord. Help me see past any inconveniences I may have to experience. Let my thoughts and motives be pure and untoward. Help me see the whole picture and choose most lovingly for all concerned. I want to deal out to others respect and courtesy. Give me your tactful presence and your graciousness so that I might communicate lovingly and with gentle care. I am so new at gauging the subtle nuances associated with mothering in the public forum. Others may not appreciate my choices; in fact, my own decisions are sure to offend some. Yet I must not fret over these impasses. I must take time and care to decide and then let it go. I am not mothering in order to win a popularity contest. I must weigh the evidence and decide with confidence in all areas. This is where I most need your assistance. I cannot rely upon my own trumped up knowledge or wisdom; I require your input each hour, every day. Nurture my heart and soul to be sensitive to your leading in all areas so as not to offend unnecessarily. Tend to my stubborn and sometimes callous heart, Lord. Remake me into a loving, sensitive soul who longs for nothing more than to bring goodness and comfort to all. Amen.

Praying to be blessed? Or praying to be a blessing?
—JOHN SLOAN IN *The Barnabas Way*

17

Deep Breath, Please

Lying on her left side, Carolyn tried to mimic her Lamaze instructor's breathing technique. Most of the in-out patterns she had no trouble mastering. But just as she was finally getting the rhythm of it, Carolyn's husband, Greg, interrupted her concentration and corrected her— again. "No, Honey, like this," he explained. Enough, Carolyn wanted to scream. I'm doing my level best here. As her ever-expanding tummy testified, Carolyn was carrying twins. She was struggling through both the days and nights now. It was uncomfortable when she sat down, never mind trying to get back up again. She hurt when she stood too long, but she felt exhausted from lying around, too. Sleeping didn't happen much these days, not with two squirming babies inside. Then there was Greg, Carolyn's overexuberant spouse and labor coach. Carolyn was about ready to shoot the man. No matter where they were headed, Greg had to painstakingly detail any news flashes he had run across in his predelivery research. It had been cute—at first. Now Carolyn had more statistics and figures stuffed in her brain than she ever thought possible. Her once-patient demeanor had taken flight about the same time she lost her waistline.

No doubt about it, just about everything Greg said brought silent disapproval from Carolyn. During those rare moments when she wasn't concentrating on finding a semi-comfortable position, Carolyn worried about her relationship with Greg. *Here we are*, she thought miserably, *close to delivering two babies into the world, and we can't even get along through a single Lamaze class without snipping at one another. What was it that my cousin told me? "Tensions ease once a baby takes its first breath." That's my hope and my prayer.*

Already he who reaps is receiving wages, and is gathering fruit for life eternal; that he who sows and he who reaps may rejoice together.
—JOHN 4:36

Dear Lord, we're at the count-down stage now, and I'm feeling the pressure from within and without. Every thought of my day is somehow connected to this upcoming delivery. I try to keep my mind on other things. But it doesn't work. My body won't allow me to be distracted for long. Each time I move, I am sorely reminded that my body is working overtime to bring two little ones into our world soon. A part of me is so ready for this to be over. But I admit to feeling some trepidation as well. Not only do I harbor questioning thoughts concerning my ability to parent, I am fearful that my husband and I have lost the closeness we once cherished. My heart, mind, and soul are so focused on getting through this pregnancy that I do not have the energy to invest in my

*marriage now. There, I said it. I know this attitude is wrong.
I must muster up some reserve of time and energy to reac-
quaint myself with my spouse. Lord, help us both weather
these changes. I realize our lives will soon be forever altered.
But I never expected the changes to occur before our family
arrived! How can this be? I am already torn between the love
for my unborn babies and my husband. My mother's heart is
beating strong as I nurture and prepare for their arrival. As
excited as we both are, we have drifted apart. Please show us
how to continue to build a strong and viable marriage. Let
nothing, not even family, bring division or dissension
between us. Be our faithful guide through these new waters
of parenting. Demonstrate to us, slow learners that we are,
the best and wisest paths to tread. Keep us tender toward one
another. Infuse your bountiful and measureless patience into
our hearts. Reward us with your continual presence, I pray.
Each day, let us never neglect to give thanks and offer up
prayers of gratitude for our relationship. And may we consistently show our love for one another despite stress, exhaustion,
and tension. Your grace is what we require. Continue your
good work within us both, and teach us the value of persist-
ence and perseverance. I commit my marriage and my family
into your care and keeping. Amen.*

*Process versus duration. Being changed within rather that rote
action without. Authenticity over quantity.*
—CAROLYN AND CRAIG WILLIFORD IN *Faith Tango*

18

Separate Ways

When Tina picked up her screaming one-year-old, husband Seth groaned audibly. Why don't you let her cry it out? Seth suggested. Tina felt torn. He just doesn't understand, and probably never will. Without an answer, Tina headed into another room and tried rocking her child back to sleep. As she swayed back and forth, back and forth, Tina felt herself settle down a bit. She could also sense her daughter relaxing and begin to lazily drift back off into sleep. After about twenty minutes of this soothing, quiet motion, Tina knew it was safe to carefully slip out of the chair and ease her young one under her comforter in the crib. But Tina refused to budge. Why should I? she thought sadly. I know the drill. As soon as I go back into the living room Seth will tell me for the umpteenth time that I need to put more priority on our relationship and spend time with him. I don't think I'm up to another such talk, Tina decided. I'd much rather sit right here and enjoy a few more tranquil moments with my daughter than be harassed into choosing my spouse's needs over those of my child.

The longer Tina sat, the more agitated she became. What had started out as a practical way to help her child transition back into sleep had now turned into a silent war between her and Seth. Tina knew he was waiting for her to come back out, and no doubt waiting impatiently as she stalled. Deliberately, Tina decided she better get it over with or Seth would take it upon himself to see what was detaining her. Slowly, Tina repositioned her child and gently laid her down in her crib. She stood gazing at her beloved daughter for only a moment more, wanting to extend the peace she felt. It was a moment too long, Tina decided, as she heard the kitchen door open and shut and then the roar of an engine start up. Instead of anger welling up, for the first time in many days, Tina cried out to God for help, and she prayed it would come swiftly.

What is the source of quarrels and conflicts among you? Is not the source your pleasures that wage war in your members? You lust and do not have; so you commit murder. And you are envious and cannot obtain; so you fight and quarrel. You do not have because you do not ask.
—JAMES 4:1–2

Dear Lord, I am sickened into the deepest recesses of my being. I grieve the changes that have developed in my relationship with my spouse. Everything that should have been wonderful with the birth of our child has turned sour. I don't believe any area of our lives remains unscathed. Lord, this is so painful. I do not think I can stand living in such an atmosphere of tension and stress. This is killing my spirit. My very soul aches with the agony of such unresolved anger.

Is there anything more I can say or do to turn this situation around? I'm at a loss. I've tried to apologize and I've asked forgiveness more times than I can count. Still, the undercurrent of anger simmers right below the surface. . . . It is the only emotion that we have in too great abundance. I am without hope.

Lord, I am at the end of myself. I desire reconciliation yet my faith is so shaken, so tenuous that it seems impossible for true healing to take place. Yet I must be willing to stick with this and persist until we reach the other side. What would I tell my child were the roles reversed? Please forgive me, Lord, for my selfish, stubborn, and resistant attitude. Of late, I've only demanded my own rights. I feel I am owed, so I demand. Please undertake in my hardened heart to soften my spirit. Remake me again into the woman whose heart is great with tenderness and compassion. Break the bonds of pride that hold me back from making a wrong right. And continue to wash me clean with your forgiving grace. I beg of you to create in me a clean heart, a new heart. Amen.

The truth is, life is filled with bedlam and blessings. It is both blemished and beautiful. Can we find the inner strength to embrace it all?
—KAREN SCALF LINAMEN IN *Sometimes I Wake Up Grumpy . . . and Sometimes I Let Him Sleep*

19
Costly Investment

Perusing the aisles of the discount store, Maddie went looking for the cheapest diapers available. After inadvertently gushing over the cost of the name brand types, Maddie decided to try an off-brand first. Next on her list came baby wipes, topical ointment, and an assortment of canned baby food. "My word, is this adding up," she murmured. Maddie couldn't believe the cost of these incidentals. After her run to the second-hand clothing store, Maddie had spent over fifty dollars outfitting her one-year-old daughter with enough winter items to last through the cold season. She hadn't counted on spending so much on the consumptive items, too. Shaking her head, Maddie tried to decide which of the baby food brands gave her the best deal for her money. But they were all different sizes, so it was difficult to compare. Here is where my latent math skills would come in handy, she said tiredly.

Discouraged and overwhelmed, Maddie paid for her purchases and then slumped into the seat of her car. She felt that familiar knot of tension in her gut tighten as she mentally calculated the total spent on this necessary shopping spree. Not much left for regular groceries, she lamented. I don't know what I was thinking. After having been blessed with three baby showers, Maddie hadn't needed to go shopping for her daughter until quite recently. Among the showers, Maddie had received enough baby clothes for the entire first year of her baby's life, boxes upon boxes of diapers, wipes, and other essential items. She had nursed too, so Maddie never purchased so much as a can of formula. But the generous supply was running low and Maddie hated to sound like a complainer, but after this last shopping expedition, Maddie realized she and her husband would have to spend some more time reworking their budget, a feat to try even the most stalwart of hearts. Though feeling a bit overwhelmed, Maddie's attention shifted when she heard a gurgle from the backseat and spied her daughter blowing raspberries as she pointed one finger out the window. Delighted by her daughter's antics, Maddie's heart lifted and she realized her precious baby was worth all they had and more.

Consider the ravens, for they neither sow nor reap; and they have no storeroom, nor barn; and yet God feeds them; how much more valuable you are than the birds!
—LUKE 12:24

Dear Lord, I'm feeling so vulnerable today. I had to face the fact that we are living within a budget that may not supply all our needs. I admit to feeling anxious and nervous about this. Never before have I had to pick and choose so carefully. It makes me feel literally sick inside when I am forced to select between two needed items. Help me let go of the tension I'm holding inside. You know all my needs. You are acutely aware of everything we must have to live. Yet despite your past faithfulness I struggle to lay my burdens down and trust you for today's needs. Forgive me, I am a woman of little understanding. Enlarge my vision and let me live this life with a strong, resilient faith. Help me overcome small obstacles and recognize temporary setbacks as opportunities to allow you to show yourself strong in my life. I am not in control of the happenings that sometime threaten to drag me under. You alone are able to see me safely through and to the other side.

Be my guide and adviser, temper my wants and desires. Fill me to overflowing with your presence and let godly contentment be my joyous companion. Help me be a conduit of thankful contentedness to my spouse. And let not temporary discouragements limit my ability to find satisfaction in my relationship with you. I pray that my countenance and my words display your love and grace to all I meet. Bless me with your perspective and keen perception of what is of true value in this life. Above all, stay close to me, continually reminding me of your ever-present hand of help that is always at the ready to lift me up when I stumble. Amen.

A child asks for breakfast in utter confidence that it will be provided. He has no need to stash away today's pancakes for fear none will be available tomorrow—as far as he is concerned, there is an endless supply of pancakes.
—RICHARD J. FOSTER IN *Celebration of Discipline*

20

By Grace I Stand

On either arm, Haley was carrying a diaper bag, her purse, and a large tray of Christmas cookies. Below her hemline, Haley's daughter, Emily, was hanging on to Haley's nylons—or more accurately, pulling and clawing at them—as she attempted in vain to gain her bearings enough to stand on her own. At eighteen months old, Emily was still not walking. Was Haley concerned? Yes. Had she spoken to her daughter's pediatrician about Emily's development? Yes. Was there any apparent reason why Emily wasn't yet toddling around on her own two feet? No. As far as Haley was concerned, she was doing everything in her power to see that Emily received any and all the medical care she needed. The refrain Haley heard over and over was, not to worry. Kids develop differently. So after several times of hearing her physician offer reassuring words, Haley did relax. Still on the alert, to be sure, but much more at ease about the situation.

What Haley didn't want or need was the nosy attention from her church's resident expert on everything from getting pregnant to getting buried. Haley stiffened, only in part due to Emily's squirming, as she spied this curmudgeon heading her way. Offhandedly, Haley was told that she most certainly should have Emily looked at by a doctor. "She has been."

"Why isn't that child walking yet?" the curmudgeon asked. "No idea," was Haley's reply. "Any developmental problems you're aware of?" "None." "Hmmm." When the flash flood of questions retreated, Haley handed off her cookies and excused herself from the line of fire. *Simmer down, Haley* breathed, *I know I've done all that I can, so do you Lord, and that's all that really counts.*

For of His fulness we have all received, and grace upon grace.
—JOHN 1:16

Dear Lord, here I am again. Forced to come before you in a spirit of abject despair and frustration. Oh, why do I allow myself to get so worked up over such inconsequential things? I am fully capable of making decisions and taking good care of my child. I do not need the furrowed brows and insinuations of self-appointed experts giving me the once over. Lord, help! I feel so undone by this latest episode of "twenty questions." I truly don't mind discussing personal issues relating to my child with others. I've learned so much from interacting with those more experienced than myself. But I can't abide the judgmental attitude, that superior tone, that graceless condemnation. It stings. It is also so very misplaced. And yet I am no better when I react in kind to such behavior. Lord, will you give me your grace to forgive the offenses I feel so deeply? Help me set aside my grievances and truly forget them. I must learn how to handle the rude comments with a greater grace. Just as you, hour by hour, love me despite my hardened heart, my stinging retorts, and my selfishness, just so I must learn to love others. In your hand, you hold all that I need. You are love, you are grace and mercy, and you are goodness. In comparison, I am sorely bereft of any of these gifts. Please begin a new work within my heart. Teach me your ways, Lord. Lift me out of my silly thoughts set on rebuttal. I am your child, let my life be so transformed by your sacrifice for me, that wherever I go, people see you in me. I pray that you would not give up on me. I know that you are faithful. But I tend to see only my faults; I know my heart too well. It grieves even my limited mind. And yet you, who are holy, love me still. What a gift you offer, with open hands I lift them high in anticipation of your generous touch. Today, I am relinquishing my rights to myself again to your care and keeping. Amen.

We should never approach truth except in a spirit of grace, or grace except in a spirit of truth. Jesus wasn't 50 percent grace, 50 percent truth, but 100 percent grace, 100 percent truth.
—RANDY ALCORN IN *The Grace and Truth Paradox*

21

Picture Perfect

*T*rish had planned this day for months. It was a breathtakingly sunny spring morning, and today her baby was to be dedicated in their church. With over twenty-plus extended family members coming to participate in the dedication service, Trish was imagining how perfectly the day would play out. She had purchased a very special, quite pricey dress and bonnet with matching silk booties and lacey stockings for the baby to wear. She herself had a creamy linen suit and brand new pumps. Right down to her husband's matching socks, Trish had relished going over the scene in her mind countless times. They'd get outstanding family portraits done to display for years to come. A sumptuous brunch would be served immediately following the service in their home. The afternoon would be filled with friendly banter and lots of reminiscing. What memories.

As the morning unfolded, Trish was ahead of schedule as they prepared to leave for the church. She did a last-minute check on the food, and the house was in order and ready to receive their guests. "Let's go," Trish said. En route to the church, Trish's dreams of a perfect day began to unravel. The baby threw up in the car. Trish was thankful that she had thought ahead and placed a receiving blanket over her daughter's dress. No damage done. A little ruffled, Trish managed to remain calm as they unpacked the car and entered the building. As Trish carried her baby into the sanctuary, she heard a noise and immediately exited to the nursery. Too late. Baby had done her duty but the diaper hadn't fulfilled its own. "No!" Trish exclaimed. Pulling out the wipes and cleaning up the mess took a while, but the lace stockings were done for. Trish wasn't about to spoil her daughter's photos with stained clothing. As she rattled around looking for a replacement pair, Trish heard the organ music begin. Hurrying, she managed to catch the lace with her wedding ring just as the baby burped up her breakfast. "Oh, what does it matter now!" Trish said in exasperation. Just then, Trish's husband peeked his head around the corner and scolded Trish for holding everything up. With a venomous look, Trish silenced her bewildered spouse and marched her soon-to-be dedicated child up the aisle, determined to salvage the day. And just one look into her darling baby's eyes as Trish held her close during the ceremony did the trick.

And looking at him, Jesus felt a love for him, and said to him, "One thing you lack: go and sell all you possess, and give to the poor, and you shall have treasure in heaven; and come, follow Me."
—MARK 10:21

Dear Lord, I want to confess that my attitude of late has been all wrong. I've been oh so concerned with presenting the pristine image of a family that has it all together. I so longed for the perfect day that would spotlight my child, Lord, that I completely missed the point. I was so busy, so vainly preoccupied with presenting a spotless illusion that I neglected to prepare my soul for this momentous event. I lost the meaning of it all by focusing on the unimportant and the temporal. Please forgive me, Lord. I see now that all my preparations were concentrated on the outward, not the inward. This was wrong. And now I can never reclaim that moment in time. Lord, help me take this foolish mistake and turn it into a lesson that will stay with me. I desire to lead my child in your ways. I want to teach her to look to you for her self-worth, her value, and her purpose. I realize I have much to learn in this area myself. Will you walk me through and be my instructor once more? I am truly overcome with shame as I consider how far I traversed from the single purpose of dedicating our child to you. For you. Remake me, heart, mind, and soul. Cleanse me from that which beckons me away from your presence. I pray these things for the sake of your son. Amen.

> *Many of us attempt, often desperately and at great cost, to be outwardly renewed day by day, while inwardly we waste away.*
> —MARK BUCHANAN IN *Things Unseen*

PART THREE

Different Dreams

*I*t is much simpler to approach motherhood sporting rose-colored glasses replete with childhood memories of how wonderful it was way back when. Yet life as a mother is rarely so idealistic. Careers are often put on hold, children are born with disabilities, others die before their time, extended families contribute negatively rather than making a positive difference. Around every bend, life throws mothers another curve ball. Rather than anticipating inevitable troubles and trials, wise moms learn how to adapt to the unexpected by depending upon the bountiful provision of God and embracing an extra measure of his mercy and grace.

22

A Real Mess

Standing under the showerhead, Mary resolved not to come out until she was thoroughly calm or the hot water ran out. Mary realized the latter was the more likely scenario. After having survived a morning of mishaps, stay-at-home mom Mary felt frazzled, undone, and like a complete failure. The night before, Mary had with good intentions made out a to-do list for the following morning. It was a tad too exacting, Mary discovered ruefully. With ten tasks to be accomplished before early afternoon naps, Mary soon admitted she'd been outrageously naïve to think she'd even tick off three of the ten by bedtime.

Frustrated at her circumstances and upset that every time she attempted to tackle a job her preschooler cried or the baby needed tending, Mary's patience level was hitting an all-time low. Not again, Mary groaned, when yet another interruption threatened to overthrow her sanity. The telephone rang, her son threw his food on the floor, and the baby smelled. "Enough already," Mary said aloud. Phone still ringing, son now playing in food on the floor, and baby wailing, Mary sat down dejectedly and felt the tears roll down her own cheeks. "What's wrong with me?" Mary cried out. "I can't even manage to keep this house clean anymore. Every time I try to get organized, I'm called upon to take care of the kids. Something's not right with this picture. It's not that I'm looking to become a Martha Stewart wanna-be, I'd just be grateful to complete some small task once I start it."

Before Mary could bemoan the challenges facing her any longer, Mary spied her goopy son trying to feed the floor-strewn food to the baby, and she ran to intervene. Well, let's just pray that no one comes knocking on my door anytime soon. Then Mary remembered, she was supposed to be delivering a meal to a new mom from her church that afternoon. The meal and good wishes I can handle, Mary laughed ironically, but she'd better not ask how my morning went!

But examine everything carefully, hold fast to that which is good.
—1 THESSALONIANS 5:21

Dear Lord, my thoughts are in such disorder I don't even know if I can articulate how I'm feeling right now. My mind is cluttered with disappointments and desires left unfulfilled. I'm unable to complete any task, no matter how insignificant. I know that my family's needs must come before other pursuits right now, but I'm stymied by my own goals. I want to stay on top of my responsibilities; I desire to be an effective and efficient manager of my home. Yet those I'm trying to serve constantly interrupt me. Lord, will you reveal to me what is most important, most valuable? I try and try to see life through your perspective, but I'm losing this battle as well. Show me the importance of what I do each day as I seek to love my children. Help me grasp the fact that a wasted day isn't equated with a day when I haven't been able to complete all my work. By Jesus' example, let me soak in the truth that people matter most. Only what I invest in my loved ones' lives will stand the test of time. Still, give me the creativity I need to discover ways to care for my family and my home as well. There are so many outside voices beckoning me to get involved in other pursuits, and I recognize at this time my energy reserves must be carefully guarded. I need your good sense to say no when requests are made that threaten the well-being of my family. Show me your ways; let my life bring honor to your name. I come to you now, needy and broken down. Please replenish my spirit both generously and completely. Amen.

> *He invites us to draw near to Him in our lumpy, unfinished, imperfect states. We don't need to have accomplished anything or overcome our weaknesses. We may have just yelled at the kids and kicked the dog.*
> —ANN KROEKER IN *The Contemplative Mom*

23

The Opposite Sex

Leah was born into a family with four brothers. Her husband was the middle-born of three boys. Her father was the eldest of six males that included a set of twins. On either side of the family, the male sex clearly predominated. So it was no surprise to Leah when she gave birth to twin boys herself. Growing up with and surrounded by boys, Leah never felt comfortable with the idea of raising girls. When friends would comment how nice it would be to bring a little girl into the mix, Leah would nod her head politely, but secretly she fretted that she wouldn't have a clue and was grateful she didn't have to.

Although Leah was a lovely, refined, and poised woman, she truly didn't believe she could deal with the nuances of raising girls. So it was no little task for Leah to come to grips with the fact that her latest ultrasound showed she was carrying a girl. Leah, stunned and more than a little overwhelmed, called her husband first and gave him the news. He was ecstatic. Next, Leah called her mom, she too, was overjoyed. Last, Leah made a quick phone call to her mother-in-law, who actually cried she was so thrilled. After making the calls, Leah should have felt better about the news. But she didn't. She was incredulous that even as she shared her concerns, everyone had so off-handedly told her

she'd be just fine. But they don't know, they just don't understand what I'm up against here. Leah knew her own heart,
she knew her limitations and her fears. *I feel like I'm heading into enemy territory*, she thought sadly. *Why aren't I as
happy as everyone else? Maybe I should take my cue from
my loved ones though*, Leah contemplated, *and perhaps
they've got greater insight on this than I do.*

*For I am confident of this very thing, that He who began a
good work in you will perfect it until the day of Christ Jesus.*
—PHILIPPIANS 1:6

*Dear Lord, I am coming to you in such neediness in my soul. I
am so bowed down with this burden that I cannot keep my
mind on any other concern. What is the matter with me, Lord?
Why can't I rejoice right along with the rest of my loved ones?
This news has me paralyzed by fear. I'm so unsure of my skills
and abilities as a parent that I'm unable to even focus on the
tasks at hand right before my eyes. My emotions are so threatening that I'm fighting against them with all my strength. It's as
though all my worrying and fretting has overtaken my good
sense. Lord, will you come close to me now? Will you wrap your
loving arms around me? Hold me, tight. Tell me the words I
need to hear to face my fears head-on. Give me your strength
and grace to help me overcome these challenges.*

*I know that I should be thanking you for your hand
of blessing in my life. But at this moment, thankfulness is a*

lifetime away. I do not feel grateful. I feel at loose ends and abandoned somehow. I suppose I have taken for granted all that you have already accomplished on my behalf. In truth, I know this. Lord, to this point, I've been coasting on my own strength, so comfortable and so unwilling to venture anywhere that I'm not confident. Will you please continue your good work in me? Give me a greater measure of faith to walk ahead with the assurance that you will be with me, guiding my steps, enabling me to be the mother you desire me to become. I long to gain my stride as a mom, loving my role as a nurturer and caregiver. But I see how very far I am from where I hunger to be. Do your good work in me, I beg. From this moment on, I pray that I am ever aware of your presence and that I am solely dependent upon you for all that I need. Amen.

> *Don't be discouraged by your weaknesses; determine instead to build on your strengths. Rejoice that God is at work in your life. He created you. He is developing you. And he is not finished with you yet!*
> —KAROL LADD IN *The Power of a Positive Mom*

24

Minor Inconvenience

*W*ith nursing kit in tow, Lisa headed for the ladies' restroom for the third and final time that workday. As public relations assistant, Lisa felt blessed that she could share her once full-time position with another woman in her office. As a new mom of a four-month-old baby girl, Lisa was grateful that her manager gave her the option of staying on part-time or coming back to her old position. Not wanting to be gone forty hours each week when her daughter was so young, Lisa opted for the Tuesday-and-Thursday schedule. This way, Lisa continued to keep up with what was happening in the advertising world while still remaining the primary caretaker of her baby. For Lisa it was a no-lose situation. Most days.

Lisa decided early on to continue nursing her daughter for the first full year. This meant pumping her milk at intervals while at work. Dashing away from her desk for the fifteen minutes it took to expel the milk wasn't usually a problem. Until today. When her supervisor scheduled a meeting at Lisa's normal pumping time, Lisa wasn't concerned. What's another hour either way, she shrugged. But when the meeting dragged on and on—one hour grew to over two and Lisa was getting uncomfortable and a tad nervous. She tried to keep her mind on the business at hand, but her thoughts kept straying back to her baby, and then she felt the milk let down. Fast as she was, it wasn't quick enough, her silk blouse showed the telltale signs of having recently given birth. Making a hasty exit, Lisa grabbed her jacket she left hanging over her chair, surreptitiously put it on, and headed for the ladies room. Red-faced and embarrassed, Lisa didn't think anyone else had noticed, still, she knew. And she wondered if the sacrifices she made to get to work were indeed worth the effort. Then Lisa stopped herself cold and reminded herself that life takes unexpected twists whether we're in the home or out of it.

The plans of the heart belong to man,
But the answer of the tongue is from the Lord.
—PROVERBS 16:1

Dear Lord, thank you for being near to me today. Even though I had my first reckoning with reality as a working mom, I sensed you were with me. I cannot admit to being glad I was placed in such an uncomfortable position. But looking back, I think you're enabling me to face even embarrassments that once would have devastated me. I'm learning to simply get into gear and handle whatever is needed with more confidence than I used to do. I'm thinking, Lord, that perhaps being a mom has instilled in me the strength and stamina to press through the tough moments. My perspective,

I'm certain, has changed as well. Thanks to you, I see the bigger picture. No longer is my job my life. I can continue to function effectively and contribute significantly, but when I walk out the door, the most important part of my day awaits me. Being with the people I love most dearly is what I count of highest value.

Thank you for allowing me to come full circle. You alone know how afraid I was to even enter into motherhood. Yet you stood with me, encouraging me and supporting me through those early weeks. Even now, as I reenter the workplace, you are with me. I cannot express how reassuring it is to sense your stalwart presence near me. It's true that my heart continues to be torn over my choice. I daily ask myself whether I've made the right decision. I'm trusting that you will continue to work within my heart as the days pass. Give me that keenness of insight and sensitivity to hear your voice. Teach me how to listen and truly hear what you're calling me to do. And prepare my heart to receive and obey. Again, I praise you for your faithfulness to me. My heart's desire is to bring honor to you through my life, no matter where those working hours are spent. Amen.

God restored us to life through Christ. Then He gave us the task of helping others be reconciled and restored spiritually. That is our spiritual job, which overlays everything we do.
—JERRY WHITE IN *Making Peace with Reality*

25

Detour Ahead

Grace stood in line at the bookstore waiting her turn to place an order for coffee. Decaf, for now. As she reached for the cup, Grace felt its warmth seep into her chilled hands and unreasonably experienced a small portion of comfort from it. Perusing the book aisles, Grace started her search for pregnancy and child-rearing books. So many to choose from that Grace was astonished; this is big business, she thought. After another forty or so minutes of browsing, Grace made her selections, paid for her purchases, and then sat down to read for a bit. She didn't want to go home, not yet. How could she tell Rodney she was finally pregnant? After ten years of marriage, Grace had conceived. Perfect timing, right? Grace felt the tears well up in her eyes as she thought about last evening's argument. Like most evenings these days, Grace and her husband spent their after-work hours either bickering over minor inconsequential topics or in silence. She didn't know which scenario she preferred. Grace abhorred conflict, so it was frequently her sudden withdrawal that hastened an ending to their verbal sparring. Still, being silent for days on end didn't solve their problems either. What to do? At this juncture, Grace wasn't sure. A month ago, Grace believed she would be divorced before the year was out. But she and Rodney had agreed to work through their differences.

But that had been before she had gotten pregnant. Grace knew that Rodney had long ago stopped hoping she would conceive. In fact, he had given up before she had. Having grown up in a large family, Rodney always dreamed of having a family that went way beyond the socially correct 2.2 children. Still, he was the first to let the dream die. When Grace suggested seeing specialists or opting for adoption, Rodney was firmly resistant. She wondered now, after having weathered so many hurts and disappointments, if their marriage was up to the added pressure of bringing a child into the world. As Grace fingered the embossed cover of her book, she realized that even if Rodney didn't choose to stay with her, she would raise her baby alone and do so gladly.

His divine power has granted to us everything pertaining to life and godliness, through the true knowledge of Him who called us by His own glory and excellence.
—2 PETER 1:3

Dear Lord, my heart is full. I feel so blessed that you have given me the desire of my heart at last. Finally, I am to be a mother. I cannot express my joy and gratefulness. Yet another part of me is grief-stricken. How can I raise this little one in a home filled with so much strife? My marriage has hit upon hard times, Lord. There have been countless days and nights when I fully believed it would not last the next twenty-four hours. This is so ironic. All these years, I've desired a family. Now, when I am realizing this dream, I have no one to share it with. Please undertake for me now. Help me grasp your eternal perspective. Let me see beyond the current tidal waves of pain and disappointment. Give me the grace I require to let loose all my anger and bitterness and put an end to my quarrelling heart. Release me from the stubbornness and pride I so frequently cling to. In my weakest moments, I too, want to give up. Lord, I know this is not your plan. You have promised to provide for my every need. Yet my circumstances contradict this. Can it be that I'm standing in the way of your provision? If I am to blame, let me humbly admit it and seek reparation with those I've injured. Demonstrate to me your forgiveness and enable me to seek the same from my loved one. Give me your grace to continue trying and let me not give in to weariness. Rather, abide with me and teach me day by day how you would have me live. I am unsure and certainly overwhelmed. But in my heart, I know this to be true. Whatever you begin, you will see through to its completion. Be it so, even now, even amidst my broken existence. I will believe in you and in your power to prevail. Amen.

If God be your partner, make your plans large.
—*God's Little Devotional Journal for Women*

26

Two Views

*T*erri picked up her Bible and daily devotional and sat down to read. "Ooh," she cried uncomfortably. "Every time I sit down, you protest," Terri gently spoke to her unborn baby. "Maybe, like me, you need more room?" Settling into a more horizontal position, Terri began reading. Sometime later, Terri set aside her Bible and book and looked over her prayer list tucked into the back of a journal. How long has it been since I've really spent time interceding for these specific needs, she wondered. A week, two, longer? Without expecting to, Terri's gaze hit upon that portion of the list most precious to her personally. Under the heading, "Faith," Terri noted her husband's name right at the top. Feeling that surge of remorse hit her, Terri held back the tears.

When she married a few years back, Terri didn't think too much about her faith, she was too busy living, having fun, and working her way through college. When Steve came around, the little concern Terri had for marrying someone of like beliefs was perfunctorily set aside. In truth, Terri hadn't given God much space in her life until she became pregnant. Then, all those thoughts about eternity and living a life that supercedes one's own interests took center stage in Terri's thoughts. She realized she wanted

Steve to share her faith. She needed him to support her efforts in raising their child in the church. Terri shouldn't have been shocked when Steve told her in no uncertain terms that he never had, and likely would never have, any interest in getting up early the one day of the week he might sleep in to attend a religious service. That's all he sees it as: some outward obligatory show. He just doesn't understand, but perhaps in time, like me, he'll start to see that it's not about religion, but rather about a relationship.

Do not fear or be dismayed because of this great multitude, for the battle is not yours but God's.
—2 CHRONICLES 20:15B

Dear Lord, how dare I come into your presence begging for help when I'm the one responsible for this problem? I knew going into this relationship that I was not of like mind with my spouse. Yet I went full ahead, not stopping to pause or consider how my actions might one day affect me. Now, not only is my choice shaping my life, it will certainly affect my child's. I feel such sadness, Lord. I allowed so many other things to take precedence over my relationship with you. I admit it now. I was so very remiss and selfish of me, only concerning myself with whatever affected my life in the present. I feel a very tangible grief settle deep within me each time my thoughts turn to this problem. I am living at an impasse with someone I love so very much. Yet I see no way through this struggle. I am often giving way to fears about future events and how my child will suffer because of my choice made so long ago. Help me now, Lord. I realize I don't deserve your compassion. Still, only to you do I turn. It will be by your strength alone that we will find common ground on this issue of faith. Please engage our hearts and minds toward you. Reveal yourself to us and let us recognize your good hand of blessing in our lives. Teach us what it means to be a follower of yours, to give our best to you. I pray that you will never stop working within our hearts. Don't give up on us. Have mercy upon me for the wrong I have done. And please protect my child despite our weaknesses. Embrace this little one with your constancy and care. Never let our negligible faith hinder our child from growing strong in you. I commit my family into your care and keeping, now and for the remainder of our days. For your glory and honor, do I ask these things. Amen.

> *I am humbled to understand that only God's tender love can take the ash out of my life—the failures, the repeated sins of addiction, the damaging relationships, the hateful words and actions—and transform them into something healthier, something that can bring glory and honor to His name.*
> —CYNTHIA SPELL HUMBERT IN *Deceived by Shame, Desired by God*

27

The Perfect Child

Natalie stooped down to help her three-year-old "tie" her Velcro-designed tennis shoes. While little Annie wasn't quite dexterous enough to handle the sturdy, cumbersome straps, she gave it all her attention and concentration. This fact alone amazed Natalie, for when Annie was born and in short order diagnosed with mild Down syndrome, Natalie felt overcome by grief for her newborn. Bombarded with medical information and seemingly nonstop phone conversations and visits with health care specialists, Annie was put on a very specific track to help her daughter develop to her fullest potential. Often weary from the mental and physical paces that were recommended for Annie, Natalie breathed a tenuous sigh of relief once she learned enough to settle into a more quiet routine on her own at home.

Two months past Annie's third birthday, Natalie was pregnant. Despite Annie's limitations and the possibility of giving birth to another baby with Down syndrome, Natalie was thrilled to have conceived again. She could hardly contain her enthusiasm and spent much time preparing Annie for the arrival of her new sibling. Together, they picked out colors for new comforters and wallpaper borders. Natalie and Annie spent many an afternoon in the baby's room folding Annie's old baby clothes and arranging things just

so. Still, with all the time spent in making practical preparations, Natalie wasn't confident that Annie was making the
connection between the baby growing within her and the
infant's room filled with baby paraphernalia. So Natalie
continued trying to make Annie "see." Whatever concerns
Natalie had about Annie's understanding of her pregnancy
vanished when Annie spotted another woman holding a
baby at their church. She pointed to the infant and then
pulled Natalie over and gently stroked her burgeoning
tummy with such love and understanding that Natalie
could have cried. She did understand. Annie might be limited in some ways, but love was not one of them.

*From childhood you have known the sacred writings which are
able to give you the wisdom that leads to salvation through
faith which is in Christ Jesus.*
—2 TIMOTHY 3:15

*Dear Lord, will there ever come a time when my first reaction
won't be one of mistrust and doubt? I wonder. All through the
years you have proven yourself faithful, just, and true to me.
My life has been encompassed by your goodness and provision.
How I have come to marvel at the mystery of your ways. It is
true that I have frequently questioned your wisdom in the
midst of the pain that seems a "must-have" on the path to
maturity. There have been times when I have wanted to
run away from the path set for me. My stubbornness and my*

self-will have caused me no end of distress. Still, you woo me back, and I finally discover and accept the grace you offered from the beginning. My hands held out, I greedily grasp your bounteous goodness, knowing I cannot face my struggles without it.

Even now, facing a new juncture in my life, I am filled with conflicting thoughts and emotions. I have been so blessed with one child and now am ready to bring another into our family. Lord, will you stretch forth your arms of strength and compassion once more? Will you extend your constancy and care toward me again? I admit to feeling somewhat apprehensive. I am trying to stem the waves of anxiety that threaten me even now. I want to be a woman of faith, of calmness, and of peace. I desire to live my life without inner fears squelching my courage and robbing my joy. Help me once again, Lord. Surround me with your love and let me walk daily basking in the light of your presence. Be my ever-present help. As I wrestle with the future unknowns, let the joy of your love reign supreme over all. I need your instruction and guidance as I continue walking this road of motherhood. Even as I see changes looming, be with me, and nurture my weak spirit into a vibrant and strong soul. Let my growing faith and my song of praise be pleasing to you. Amen.

There are certain passions only learned by pain. And there are times when God, knowing that, allows us to endure the pain for the sake of the song.
—MAX LUCADO IN *A Gentle Thunder*

28
Clockwatcher

Working like a fiend, Ali drummed out five replies to her on-line students. Later, after a quick lunch break, I'll tackle the remaining forty-five, she sighed. Maybe, just maybe, I can get them done before the baby wakes up from his nap, Ali thought wishfully. You never know, it just might happen, she answered herself back. Halfway through a chicken salad sandwich, Ali heard her little Addison's murmuring cries slowly grow into a roar of discontent. "OK, OK, I'm coming," she mumbled as she gobbled up the last vestiges of lunch. Wiping the crumbs from her fingers, Ali swiftly rinsed and loaded her cup and plate into the dishwasher, washed her hands, and bounded into her son's room. By now, exactly two and one half minutes after waking up, Addison was screaming, his normally pink-toned skin blotchy and red. "It sure doesn't take you long to rev up your engines, does it little guy?"

A quick diaper change and a late lunch for the baby took Ali about twenty minutes. After every bite Addison swallowed of his applesauce, Ali longingly gazed at her computer screen. She could almost hear it calling her name. Never one to put off work, Ali was having a tough time ordering her at-home workday around caring for the baby. An ambitious young woman, Ali never missed a beat when she accepted the job to teach an on-line high school course from home. Little did she realize how many e-mails she would receive on a daily basis from her students. It was disheartening to click on the computer screen and see just how little these young people seemed able to accomplish independently. They were either confused about the directions or didn't have the skills to complete the ones they understood. Ali diligently tried to squeeze in the time for them and for Addison. The family needed the income and she loved her work. So Ali was determined to continue trying one tack after another to find the most effective method for accomplishing all she was called to do.

Yet you do not know what your life will be like tomorrow. You are just a vapor that appears for a little while and then vanishes away.
—JAMES 4:14

Dear Lord, a little perspective here would be well received right now. I'm finding myself watching the clock and glancing at my wristwatch in tired frustration all throughout the day. I am so out of focus, Lord, I cannot even enjoy the time spent with my child. I admit to feeling pressed on every side by demands and deadlines. And I understand that my current circumstances are of my own making. Yet I truly believed I could handle it all. Never once did I suspect the time and energy required to care for one small baby. I realize now how naïve I was. But I desired the best of both worlds. I have always loved my career and I grieved to give it up. Now I am sincerely torn each and every day as I attempt to give my best to both of these endeavors. Can I do it? Will I find a way to make it work out? I know now that without your good hand of guidance I stand no chance of being successful as a mother and as a working woman. Please help me streamline my life as much as possible. Help me funnel out the unnecessary distractions that threaten my sanity. Demonstrate to my limited mind what is of true and lasting value. Let my life be invested only in that which will endure. Lord, I am weary from the endless work. I am exhausted in every way conceivable. Still, I am not willing to give up. I believe you can show me how to manage my life more efficiently and effectively. Will you please make up for my lack? Give me what it is I need for today. Balance my expectations and make them reasonable and not prone to excessiveness. Be my conscience that speaks to the deepest recesses of my heart, Lord. Let me live each day with a keen awareness of the finiteness of life and an appreciation for all the blessings bestowed upon me. Amen.

> *Take time for make-believe. Abandon yourself in play. I think God gives us an imagination for a reason. Christ knows the pressures we endure. Perhaps this is one reason he encourages us to "become like little children."*
> —JEAN LUSH IN *Women and Stress*

29

A New Tradition

After drifting off during the evening news, Nancy awoke with a start at nearly 9:00 P.M. She sat up abruptly and changed channels. I almost missed it, she chided herself. Flipping to the correct station, Nancy stopped, and took notice. This was it, the program Nancy had read about earlier in the week, the one television special she had to see. While Nancy rarely watched TV, tonight was the exception. The health channel was running a series on alcohol- and drug-related illnesses. Nancy, a nonsmoker, nondrinker, and abhorrer of any type of prescription or nonprescription drugs, had good reason for taking special interest in this program. Her own mother, a self-confessed alcoholic- and prescription-drug addict, had died when Nancy was just a kid. Nancy could still remember the painful aftermath that followed one of her mother's binges. Her father would rant, they would argue, a door would slam, leaving Nancy alone in the house with her drunken mother. Although her mom didn't pull any outrageous stunts while intoxicated, she did injure Nancy emotionally, over and over again. Nancy felt the strange pull to "mother" her mom during these episodes. It was far too much pressure for an eleven-year-old to handle. Then, to add insult to injury, Nancy's mom overdosed one night. Nancy was thankful that her father, not Nancy, had found her mom, but Nancy could never seem to find closure from her all too agonizing childhood.

As a married woman, now expecting, Nancy found herself waking up in the middle of the night, her heart beating out of her chest. Nancy knew better than to believe she'd follow in her mother's footsteps. Still she wondered how her mother had spiraled into such a desperate state. Had her mother always struggled with substance abuse? Where did it come from? Why had it started? When no answers came, Nancy would wrestle with her own private fear of some as yet unexposed character weakness that would suddenly make its appearance and destroy her life as it had her mother's. Finally Nancy decided to be proactive and learn all she could about her late mother's struggles so that she could finally put her fears to rest for good.

Heal me, O Lord, and I will be healed;
Save me and I will be saved,
For Thou art my praise.
—JEREMIAH 17:14

Dear Lord, I am a wandering soul, aren't I? These days I can't seem to stay in the present. I spend far too much time looking back into a past I desperately want to forget. I believed that I had put it all behind me. It happened so long ago, but still the memories cling to me, pulling me this way and that. Lord, I want to be free of them all. Will you lead me to a place where the past cannot hurt me anymore? Envelop me within the confines of your goodness and grace. Be my protective shepherd as you help me traverse through these treacherous memories. Lord, my mind recoils when I consider all that I experienced as a child. Yet my remembrances betray me. Sometimes I can recall wonderful, happy moments. Then within seconds, after I am off my guard and in a trusting, melancholy mood, I am suddenly cringing under the burden of yet another uncalled upon memory. My past is part of my history, a part of me. Please, as your word says, make all things work together for good for those who love you. And I do love you, Lord. I am your child and thankful of it. I realize that I will always carry some memory of my pain within my heart. Forever, these happenings have served to shape me. Yet I do not believe they need hold me captive. Let me embrace the past in such a way that I use it as school of learning, serving only to help me make wise and prudent choices for my own life. Let not the mistakes of others wound me irreparably. Rather, let their failings exist as reminders to take heed of your words and walk in your ways. Heal me, Lord, make me whole. Do your miraculous work of complete and utterly magnificent restoration within my soul. As always, I wait upon you. Amen.

We must relinquish unrealistic desires for full explanations. . . . When Job demanded answers from God, he didn't get the explanations he wanted. He was instead given God's presence. Somehow this was sufficient.
—ALBERT Y. HSU IN *Grieving a Suicide*

30

Wise Ways

*L*inda sat perched next to her newborn's crib. She watched in awe as her daughter slept. What a miracle! Linda couldn't have held back the tears if she had wanted to. At this very moment, nothing on earth was as transfixing as the gentle in-out baby breaths of her child. Placing a finger near her baby's slightly parted lips, Linda felt a tingle run up her spine as the warm breaths touched her skin. Lovely, perfect, innocent, my child, Linda thought fiercely. She's a gift beyond the measuring, that much I know. Settling back in the wooden rocker, Linda had no desire to leave the nursery. She had a million tasks that needed completing. But she couldn't move. Held captive by her tiny daughter's restful repose, Linda finally closed her own eyes and drank in the sounds and smells of babyhood.

All around her, Linda was lovingly reminded of her commitment to raise her daughter in a house full of faith. She knew it wouldn't be easy, but Linda was convinced that although her own childhood had been a happy one, it had lacked the abiding presence of God. No one ever spoke to Linda about faith or Christ. Until she was older, Linda couldn't recall having ever entered a church apart from weddings and funerals. Linda smiled as she reminisced about the curious path she had journeyed to get where she was now. Round about with lots of life's hard knocks in between, Linda conceded. Still, I found my way, or perhaps more accurately, God led me here. As Linda continued to meditate on God's faithfulness to her, she felt herself uttering silent pleas for guidance and strength. Linda, having experienced so much pain in her life, wanted to protect her daughter from as many of life's hardships as possible. As soon as she sent up a petition for mercy, Linda's heart responded to God's answer. It's the struggles that sift away the dross, leaving behind the polished beauty of a heart completely surrendered to Me, a truly beautiful thing.

How blessed is he whose help is the God of Jacob,
Whose hope is in the Lord his God;
Who made heaven and earth,
The sea and all that is in them;
Who keeps faith forever;
Who executes justice for the oppressed;
Who gives food to the hungry.
The Lord sets the prisoners free.
—PSALM 146:5–7

Dear Lord, make me yours today. In heart, soul, body, and spirit, I want nothing more than to reflect your eternal love to those under my care. My heart is finally tender toward the precepts and principles of faith. Keep it this way, Lord. Let me not become hardened and resistant when difficulties arise.

Be my guide and leader through the tangled webs I'll have to traverse. I am weak and simple minded, Lord, but you know all. You see beyond my limited understanding. As a new mother, I am frequently unsure of the next step. I become easily irritated and caustic in my speech. Lord, you alone can calm me and teach me to slow down, trust in your provision, and lean upon you for all my family's needs. Yet I sometimes long to do things my way again. I refuse to listen to good counsel, both within and without. I stubbornly insist on my own way, ignoring the courteous entreaties from your spirit. Please forgive me. After all my platitudes about serving you, I continue to strive for life on my own terms. Lord, I say it with the most sincere respect: I truly want you to be Lord over my life. Your ways are perfect and best. But a part of me, the mother in me, wants to demand safety, security, and absolute protection for my child. I am most determined when I believe some harm may come to my family. Lord, will you even now help me release my loved ones into your keeping? They are in far better hands in the hands of their creator than in my feeble, fallible ones. Lord, do your work of continued sanctification within me now. Never stop this delicate, time-consuming surgery of the soul. Let my life reveal you and your love with grace and consistency. Amen.

Make me as wondrous as the stars in the sky by making me more and more Your servant. Let me reflect Your light.
—LISA TAWN BERGREN IN *God Encounter*

PART FOUR

Nurturing a Joyous Spirit

Real mothers, the ones who get up in the middle of the night when their child cries, who tend to their sick children without a complaint, who anticipate their baby's needs before any outward indication is given, these moms are the rule rather than the exception. With lives often littered with disappointment, discouragement, and countless setbacks, these mothers keep on going and keep on giving. Despite all odds, they don't give up and they don't give in. With a maternal love so strong it borders on fierce, these moms deserve immeasurable recognition and applause—but they'd never expect it.

31
Swing Shift

$\mathcal{K}$elsey had five minutes of her break remaining. She gulped down her juice, threw the remnants of lunch into the garbage container nearby, and studied her calendar. Her residency would be starting up in June and by then she'd be four months pregnant. Could she handle it? Was is wise to even try? Kelsey tore out the current calendar page and tossed it as well. "So much for wise planning," she spoke under her breath. Kelsey grabbed her purse and bag and headed back to the ER. As she walked the hospital corridors, she couldn't help but laugh at the irony of her situation. She had longed for a baby for over six years but with the diagnosis of endometriosis putting a spin on her "plans" to get through college and then start a family, everything had changed. Kelsey and her husband had tried to conceive a child ever since Kelsey had completed her nursing degree. After those six years of hoping against hope she'd become pregnant, Kelsey faced the hard truth that she may never have a child of her own.

So she opted for choice number two, become a pediatrician. Kelsey had worked herself ragged through medical school, and her final challenge, residency in the hospital where she now worked, was the last hurdle before realizing her dream. Now, pregnant? Kelsey still couldn't fathom it.

She also was struggling to find a feasible way to finish up her schooling without going out of her mind. Kelsey had heard and seen the horrors of shift upon shift that residents were required to work. She didn't know whether she could handle it and be pregnant, too. Would she somehow sacrifice her unborn child's health and her own by all those stressful and long work schedules? But how could she even consider giving up now after all she'd accomplished to get this far? *Calm down*, Kelsey chided herself, *I'll find a way—or more accurately, God will show me the way.*

Oh, the depths of the riches both of the wisdom and knowledge of God! How unsearchable are His judgments and unfathomable His ways! For who has known the mind of the Lord, or who became His counselor?
—ROMANS 11:33–34

Dear Lord, how can this be happening to me? To us? Lord, you know how greatly we have desired to conceive a child. These many years we have longed to hold our own baby and have had to endure the pain of watching others around us bear child after child. It was so very painful to continue living, hoping against hope that we might one day have our own family. Finally, we accepted the fact that this was unlikely. So certain were we that we made other plans, set new goals, and occupied ourselves with other endeavors. And this has been a good thing. But now, my heart and head are spinning. I don't know what to make of this new development. A baby? Now? My own child? This is wondrous and amazing to me. I thank you, Lord, for this blessing. My heart cannot express the joy I am feeling when I consider what miracle is developing within me. I am truly overcome and in awe of this.

Yet I'm pulled back to reality when I try to work out the best way to handle my current obligations in light of this pregnancy. Will you give me your wisdom, Lord? Help me set proper priorities within my days. Show me what you consider to be most important. I do desire to finish what I've begun, Lord. But I want to be prudent as well. Help us decide the best course to follow and let not the demands of life temper our joy. Enable us to plan with sound and careful thought to every detail. Reveal to us ways to overcome our obstacles and let us not be overwhelmed during these coming weeks and months. Prepare us fully, I pray, for this new phase of life. Instruct our hearts and lend us your love and constancy as we grow into the role of parenting. Be with us, surround us, and lead us. Amen.

We often struggle with God's plan and direction. We desire to see everything laid out nicely and neatly—where we will work, whom we will marry, what we will experience. We can develop visions for these areas of our lives, but our security is in knowing who leads the trip.

—JUD WILHITE IN *Faith That Goes the Distance*

32

Instructive Introspection

*A*nnette squeezed into the narrow, badly scarred, aging pew, wondering why today of all days she'd even think to notice such a minor detail. As she sat down, she also took note of the finely crafted stained glass windows that depicted marvelous biblical scenes. Within minutes Annette also realized another fact: there in the ninety-eight degree plus heat ran three modern-looking ceiling fans feebly moving the stifling air over many bodies, all scrunched together as uncomfortably as she. Annette suddenly realized she was examining her surroundings in a vain attempt to take the edge off her own wounded emotions as to why she sat in this church on such a blistering Thursday morning.

Just three days ago, the call had come. Annette's cousin's daughter had been killed in a car crash. At only ten years old, this child's death had literally wrung the life out of her family, friends, and, truth be told, the entire community. No wonder this church is so packed, Annette thought with tears brimming. The passing of such a young child and in such a tragic way breaks the hearts of everyone. It just isn't supposed to be. Parents should be the ones who leave this life first.

Like everyone else present, Annette's thoughts were focused on loved ones; in Annette's case, her young sons.

With two toddlers and a third on the way, Annette felt stricken. Hadn't she just called her mom yesterday to complain about not having any time alone? Hadn't she further indicted herself by taking part in a full-blown self-pity "party" after that phone conversation? And what were Annette's first words to her husband when he walked in the door last night? Something along the lines of, "Get me out of here!" Annette let the tears flow freely now. But only she knew it wasn't simply for the grief of her cousin's loss but also for her own lack of gratefulness for what she possessed.

The Lord lift up His countenance on you,
And give you peace.
—NUMBERS 6:26

Dear Lord, I'm grieved for my attitude of late. I feel so badly about my selfish small-mindedness that I am tempted to push this offence out of my mind and try to forget my failings. But you know the truth of my hardened heart already. You alone are already aware of my struggles with contentment and gratefulness. These past months, I feel as though someone has taken my very heart and squeezed it dry of any emotion. Why do I believe that my burdens are so very heavy? I wonder, how have I come to this place of such discontent that I am unable to see the blessings that are so abundant? Lord, I do need your forgiveness. How can I fail to recognize your good hand of provision and protection on me and those I love? Countless are the times when you and you alone cared for our needs in ways I can only proclaim as miraculous.

Help me step back and reassess my life. I want to nurture a thankful heart in every circumstance. I desire nothing more than the close communion we once had. I know I am the one at fault. I've been so focused on plowing through my busy days that I've not taken any time to quiet my heart and mind and nourish my spirit. Teach me to be wise in how I spend my time, and make me so very aware that the only way to build a strong faith, a faith with enough resilience to face the hardships of life, is to immerse myself in the truth of your word. Your strength alone will carry me through hard times. Lord, undertake for me today, I pray. Mold me into the woman and mother I long to be. Give me that tender touch and sensitive spirit I once held so dear. Let me learn how to love again. And, please, let me never again take for granted those whose lives I so cherish. Your good gifts are all around me. I must take the time to recognize and embrace every one. Amen.

Too many times I have offered up the prayers of a beggar, always asking for more and forgetting my thanks.
—ANDY ANDREWS IN *The Traveler's Gift*

33
The Tough Good News

Reminiscing over the long-past days of their childhood, Emma smiled. She couldn't think of better memories than those she shared with her sister, Dee. They were two of a kind. Always the same dreams and desires brewing in their minds, right along with the craziest schemes to make those pie-in-the-sky wishes a reality. Emma, the younger of the two siblings, found that as the years into young adulthood passed, she and Dee were still working to see their lifelong goals come to fruition. Like her sister, Emma became an elementary school teacher. Like Dee, Emma married at twenty-four. Both scrimped and saved and eventually moved into old rambling farmhouses barely an hour from one another. Next came assorted pets, and now babies were on the agenda. Dee and her husband had been trying to conceive a child for just over two years when Emma became pregnant. Though Emma and her spouse were thrilled, Emma dreaded telling Dee. What will she think? How can she be happy for me when she's having trouble becoming pregnant?

These thoughts and more tumbled around in Emma's brain the night before a family dinner gathering. Emma fretted to no end that Dee, while not angry, wouldn't be able to contain her own sadness at hearing Emma's news. It was a bittersweet evening of contemplation to be sure. Emma couldn't get her mind off of her pregnancy and Dee's current state of infertility. Would this dampen their closeness? Would Emma feel the need to steer clear of conversations revolving around her pregnancy? Emma wasn't certain about how this would all pan out. But she realized after hours of stewing over the matter that none of her worry was accomplishing anything worthwhile. So Emma decided to sit down and write her sister a love letter. Emma put on paper everything she was feeling. She communicated her love and commitment to Dee as well as her anxieties and fears. Then she sealed the letter and determined that she'd give it to Dee before they parted ways the next evening.

There is an appointed time for everything.
And there is a time for every event under heaven. . . .
A time to weep, and a time to laugh;
A time to mourn, and a time to dance.
—ECCLESIASTES 3:1, 4

Dear Lord, my thoughts and mind are all in a muddle. I am so thrilled that I am going to have a child. Yet another part of me is agonizing for one I love who has not been able to yet conceive. How can I feel so conflicted over this wonderful event? I am troubled in my soul. I feel as though I have wronged this dear one by getting pregnant. Lord, you know this is not so, still my heart and mind struggle to think reasonably concerning this matter. My emotions are telling me these two very opposing messages. Be happy, rejoice! Next, grief and heavy heartedness take precedence. I wonder how to make this situation easier for everyone I love. Please help me soothe any troubled hearts. If responses are not what I had hoped, give me your tender love to accept it graciously. Help me be sensitive to the disappointment in those around me and let not any of my enthusiasm injure another. Please show me the balance of expressing my joy while maintaining a caring heart toward others.

Lord, let not any spirit of division come between us. Protect our relationship. I treasure it so. Instruct our hearts to reach beyond this circumstance and let us all bring honor to you through our attitudes and actions. Give grace where it is needed. Bestow a generous supply of your support, I pray. Teach us how to esteem others higher than ourselves and let us not neglect doing good to those around us. Lord, I thank you for this new life you have brought into being at this time. Help us trust in your ways and your wisdom and your plans for each of us. I pray that my loved ones can sincerely rejoice with us. Be with us now, and mend any brokenness or heartache. Amen.

Growth in depth and strength and consistency and fruitfulness and ultimately in Christlikeness is only possible when the winds of life are contrary to personal comfort.
—ANNE GRAHAM LOTZ IN *Just Give Me Jesus*

34

Rest Stop

*K*ristin's leg cramped and her foot angled out uncomfortably as she tried to work the muscle loose. As soon as she'd massaged her calf into submission, her foot would cramp again and she'd try to lean forward to stop the pain. This is what lying in bed all day, every day, does to a body, she thought ruefully. Here I am, restricted to my bed or couch except for bathroom breaks. Kristin attempted to move into another position, but the weight of her baby made lying flat on her back impossible now. I can't breathe, she lamented. "Here we go," she murmured to herself. "Let's roll over to the left side now. OK, turn." Once she managed to change positions Kristin found herself facing the blank wall of her bedroom. Well, isn't this is just like my life right now, on hold, standstill, and stagnant. Trying to maintain a sense of calm, Kristin commanded herself to think about all the good coming from being ordered to bed by her OB.

I can catch up on my letter writing and thank-you notes from the baby shower. I can finally dig through that pile of magazines I've been collecting for the last couple of years. I might even get my photos organized and placed into albums, which would be a miracle. What else? Kristin's mind went blank. All she really wanted was to experience her first pregnancy like the majority of other new moms: active, on the go, and eagerly making preparations for the baby and the baby's nursery. But she knew what a tenuous position her baby was in. Kristin needed to rest quietly, at least for another four weeks. Otherwise, her precious child might not survive if she went into labor prematurely. Kristin grabbed her latest ultrasound photo and marveled at what she saw. "Amazing," Kristin said wonderingly. "I know you're worth any price, little one. Your mom just can't get used to this much quiet in her life. But you'll soon change all that, won't you?"

If you then, being evil, know how to give good gifts to your children, how much more shall your Father who is in heaven give what is good to those who ask Him!
—MATTHEW 7:11

Dear Lord, please speak to my discontented heart today. I am full of self-pity and even some small measure of self-loathing. I detest being constrained to a quiet existence, Lord. You know me better than anyone. As I sit alone I consider all the important tasks I might be completing were my body stronger. All those unanswerable questions loom large in my mind's eye and continue to feed my frustrations. Lord, I know that at this time I must accept my path with good grace—accept that this downtime is a gift from your hand, one to be used with wisdom and accepted gratefully. Yet so much of me is aching to get moving and get prepared for my baby. Will you help quiet my spirit? My emotions are running full speed ahead and my mind races with anticipation over all that still needs to be readied. Help me rest fully in body, mind, and spirit. Let me take full advantage of this time spent in solitude to make prayerful preparations I might not otherwise accomplish.

Calm me, Lord. Give me your peace that does indeed pass beyond all human understanding. I am in need of your soothing presence and perspective. As I feebly attempt to gain a more restful repose, speak contentment to my heart and give me a burden to work off my energy through laborious prayer. Place on my heart those you would have me intercede for, and begin instructing me in the ways of praying for my unborn child. Let me learn, early on, the power of time spent alone with you, standing in the gap for others as well as myself. Unleash your Holy Spirit to come and fill the void that threatens to overtake me. Strengthen me and support my determination to follow the path of caution during these final days of my pregnancy. Help me see past my own discomfort and understand that I am investing in the life of my child through this simple sacrifice. Let me realize that any moments spent in your presence are time well spent. Amen.

Prayer can be exhausting work, and only one person loves your children enough to bless them through prayer day after day, week after week, year after year. You.
—JEANNIE ST. JOHN TAYLOR IN *How to Be a Praying Mom*

35

In Sync

Kneading her throbbing temples didn't help, nothing did. Taylor recognized the symptoms early on. The blinding headaches, the distracted thoughts, and her trademark tip-off, her snappy tongue. It was the noise, Taylor told herself. *I just can't stand this much commotion going on all around me day in and day out. I need some quiet. Solitude is not a negotiable for me.* Taylor sighed and then cried. Although all was momentarily still in her household, soon her baby would awaken from her nap and her two-year-old would bound out of their shared bedroom as well. From then on, until well past Taylor's ability to reasonably cope, the children would be lifting the sound decibel level far beyond any sane mother's measurable limits. *I have what, maybe another twenty peace-filled minutes,* Taylor thought desperately. *What should I do in that short precious time slot,* she wondered. Spend it reading? Catch up on some bills? Make the three phone calls I should have made yesterday? Plan dinner? Clean? Do a load of laundry? Weed my forsaken rose garden?

As Taylor's weary mind considered one dreary task after another, her spirits sank even lower. *I know what I really want to do,* she decided. *I'd love to lie down and take a good long nap with the absolute assurance that no one*

will interrupt me! I really could use a full hour of total
silence to help bring my perspective back into the realm of
sanity. Lord, do I even chance it? Taylor grabbed a throw
blanket and tucked a pillow under her head. She closed her
eyes, and took several deliberately slow deep breaths. Calm
down, she told herself. Within minutes, one exhausted
mom was lazily drifting off into a quiet, restful retreat.

*Cast your bread on the surface of the waters, for you will find
it after many days.*
—ECCLESIASTES 11:1

*Dear Lord, how I would welcome some alone time right
now. I feel as though my mind will soon explode and with it
my ability to cope as a mother. I never realized what little
things would bother me most about mothering. Even though
I haven't had much experience with little ones, I always
hoped I could jump right in and parenting would become
second nature to me. In some ways, this has been true. Yet
certain very specific areas dredge up so much turmoil within
my heart that I can scarcely function. Lord, you know how I
love my children. Yet the constant crying and loud crashing,
banging, and rambunctious behavior sends my mind spinning. At times I would like nothing better than to hand these
little ones off to someone and run, fast and far. I know that
you understand my struggles. I ask you now to strengthen me
with your strength. Give me an extra measure of patience as
I strive to love my family despite my shortcomings.*

I realize that these days will be gone all too soon. Yet I am tempted to look into the future and long for my children to be older. Somehow, I can't wait to turn the next corner in parenting. I look around and see families farther along in their lives, and I envy their independence. Lord, forgive me. I know that my years as a mom will fly swiftly by. Then I'll be the one looking back and regretting. Help me appreciate this day and value my life as it is at this moment. Let me not forsake the wonders of mothering at the stage where I am right now. Clothe me with contentment and a sense of perspective that sees beyond the daily challenges. I can only accomplish this great work with your steady hand to guide and enable me. Be my constant resource of hope and vision, Lord. For your sake and the sake of these beloved children, I pray. Amen.

There are moments of glamour, days of celebration. We have our share of feasts, but we also have our share of baloney sandwiches. And to have the first, we must endure the second.
—MAX LUCADO IN *A Gentle Thunder*

36

Operation Baby

Andrea unlocked the door to her apartment, threw down her coat and purse, listened to the messages on her answering machine, and went to the kitchen to begin dinner. With the refrigerator door flung open, Andrea stared unseeingly inside, not knowing how long she stood there in frozen limbo as her cat's tail stroked her legs and wove in and out around her feet. When no response came, Andrea's cat bit her ankle. "Ouch!" Andrea yelped. Reaching down, she picked up the Persian puffball and held him close. Shutting the fridge door despondently, Andrea carried her pet to the living room and snuggled with him on the sofa. For a moment, Andrea felt the fear slip away, and she was content. No one was bothering her with tough questions, questions to which she had no answers. She decided on the way home she wouldn't answer the phone tonight either. Andrea couldn't take any more advice—probably sound advice, she admitted, but definitely not welcome. The calls left on her machine would have to be put off until another day when she was feeling stronger.

I've got about forty-eight hours to pull myself together before Mitch arrives home from his trip. So what do I say? Hey, Honey, guess what—I'm declared cancer-free and

I'm pregnant, all in one breath? Andrea shuddered. How could this be? The very last thing Andrea had expected when she went into her doctor's office that afternoon was to hear such good-bad news. The good news being she was cancer-free—the tests proved it. What a relief. But they also showed she was about eight weeks along in her first ever pregnancy. Didn't the doctors tell her that all her treatments might mess up her regular cycles? Didn't they tell her not to worry about missing a month here or there? They certainly did, and she had. Now, pregnant and after having used so many potent and potentially lethal drugs to fight her cancer, Andrea was beside herself with worry. She knew her baby's health might very well have been compromised and she had had no clue, so Andrea lay down and willed herself to consider all the wondrous ways in which God had been so faithful as she fought her cancer. *You were there with me when I fought death; I'm going to count on you while I create life.*

I lay down and slept;
I awoke, for the Lord sustains me.
—PSALM 3:5

Dear Lord, what type of prayer do I offer now? Prayer for healing and wholeness? Petitions for mercy and grace? I am amazed and distressed at the timing of such an event. How can this be? I am still recovering, still very much in the fight for my own life, and now I'm pregnant too? I wish it were not so. I do not have the strength to fight against such forces. In one part of my body an enemy fights to destroy my life, in another new life is growing. I cannot even comprehend such a thing. How do I handle such conflicts that war within me? I am honest when I say I am in despair. My mind is shutting out the pressures, my emotions are numb, even my body is slowed and still. Oh, Lord, please come to my rescue. Deliver me from this place of such overwhelming fear and darkness. I have never before been so afraid. Show me how to reclaim my faith in your ongoing and constant provision. Surround my heart and mind with promises from your word. Let me rise above this. I am cast adrift and unable to find my way back to the safety of your loving embrace. Extend yourself in my direction and take firm hold of me. Never let me go. I do not know or pretend to understand the whys behind this event. Yet in my heart of hearts I believe that you only desire good for me. With the merest thread of courage and resolve, I commit my life and that of my child's into your care and keeping. Be strong for me, Lord, be my all in all. I call upon you alone for the courage and strength I'll require to face down the enemies of my body and soul. Lead me to a safer place, a quiet, restful haven, I pray. Amen.

Relinquishment takes us into rugged terrain. The climb is steep, the rocks are sharp, and the trail passes by precarious ridges.
—RICHARD J. FOSTER IN *Prayer: Finding the Heart's True Home*

37
Vital Information

As Sonya sat in the inner waiting room with her daughter, Paige, it was all she could do not to break down into great, convulsing sobs. Her dear baby girl was ill but none of the tests had uncovered anything conclusive. Paige wasn't gaining weight, nor was she able to keep many foods down. Either Paige brought food back up or it went right through her system. In both cases, this fourteen-month-old could not be described as a thriving toddler. Sonya wondered how her physician could even describe Paige as a toddler when she couldn't walk, didn't stand, and never even pulled herself to an upright position. The very name, *toddler,* caught in Sonya's throat as a bitter reminder of how sick her daughter truly was.

As much as Sonya hated to admit it, she now wondered whether adoption had been the most prudent choice. With their state's closed adoption laws, Sonya had no access to Paige's birth parents' health history. How many times had Sonya called and pleaded with the director at the adoption agency? While sympathetic, this woman could not simply hand out personal information without the written consent of the birth parents. And who knows where the birth parents now lived? Last address, unknown. Sonya firmly believed that whatever was ailing her daughter almost certainly had some genetic underpinnings. But then again, it didn't matter what Sonya believed, there were specific, non-negotiable laws that provided no recourse to the adoptive parents.

"Which leaves me exactly where I was before," Sonya despaired, "with hands tied and no ability to taken action." At this point, she surmised, the doctors, at best, are simply guessing what's wrong. I want and need more than mere guesswork for my daughter, and the only place I know for certain I can get it is on my knees at the throne of God.

Behold, God is my salvation,
I will trust and not be afraid;
For the Lord God is my strength and song,
And He has become my salvation.
—ISAIAH 12:2

Dear Lord, give me an added portion of your saving strength and grace this day. I am bereft of hope and do not know where to turn for assistance. I cannot get the answers I need to help my child. I am fighting against forces larger and more powerful than I. Will you come to my aid? I need you as my shepherd and loving protector to guide me through these treacherous waters. It would take but a wisp of wind to topple me over at this moment. I am struggling to stay composed so that I might carry on my day's work. I am trying in vain to stem the tide of my weeping. I am undone and defeated, Lord. What more can I do? I have honestly exhausted every avenue of help I can find. If there is another untried resource, Lord, please reveal it to me. Never before have I felt so utterly helpless. Even though I have followed all the correct steps and have diligently applied the right treatments, nothing has made a difference. How alone and vulnerable I am. Please come to me now, shed your silence, and please speak to my heart. I must hear your calming voice that reassures me all will be well. I must have some guarantee of your promised help during these next days and weeks. Show yourself strong on our behalf, Lord. Let the impossible become possible. Let others see your goodness and even miraculous provision become reality. Bring your light into this dark place and let me again praise you for your faithfulness. Gird me up even now with a fresh measure of courage, and let my spirit not become brittle, but resilient and able to adapt to the ever-changing whims of circumstance. Finally, I ask that your irrepressible spirit of grace flood our hearts and strengthen us through this trial. We come to you alone, every day, every hour. Amen.

God knows everything about you. He is thoroughly aware of all the personal struggles that threaten to undo you. He knows your history and your present life, all of it. And all he says to you is, "Christ."
—LARRY CRABB IN *Finding God*

38

Remembering You

When Brenda's infant son died, Brenda didn't cry, scream, lament—anything. With an eighteen-month-old toddler in tow, Brenda watched dry-eyed as her husband Rick wept all way to the funeral director's office. After another ninety or so minutes of a grit-your-teeth-to-get-through-it session of answering questions and making decisions, both mom and dad were spent. Brenda found that as long as she was expected to contribute to the decision-making process as they prepared for little Brandon's funeral, she could function. It was after the logistics had been arranged that Brenda began struggling for composure. Brenda still couldn't comprehend how her young son had died so quickly. What was wrong with this picture? Didn't they live in the most affluent nation in the world? Didn't they have access to the finest and most advanced medical treatments? Why hadn't it been enough? Even as she asked these questions, Brenda tried to keep her emotions at bay. You're handling this so well, friends commented. Other, more astute family members were worried more for Brenda's silent acceptance than for Rick's outward and expected show of grief. In trying to cope and regain some measure of control over her life, Brenda became fixated on keeping Brandon's memory alive.

Two days before the funeral, Brenda ran out to the paper box to retrieve that morning's newspaper. Frantically, she scanned the obituary; it was crucial they got all the information down correctly. As Brenda read the listing, she felt a sudden relief. Everything was going to be all right; down to the last word, Brandon's obituary was just as they had dictated. Relief flooded through Brenda. Next, Brenda fixated on making certain the funeral went exactly according to plan. When the minister neglected to mention some of the special memories they'd had with Brandon, Brenda reacted big time by withdrawing even more. It took days for Rick to draw Brenda out and help her to see that it wasn't the end of the world. But why did it feel that way? Gently, Rick sat with Brenda and held her, and they rocked back and forth until Brenda was finally able to unleash the rush of tears she had been holding inside.

My soul is deeply grieved, to the point of death; remain here and keep watch with Me.
—MATTHEW 26:38

Dear Lord, I'm not sure I can bring together my thoughts enough to pray. Right now, everything is a mixed-up jumble. From my emotions to my heart to my mind, all are at loose ends. I am unable to connect with the people around me. I cannot comprehend how things should hold together. Lord, I realize that I am in some stage of grieving, at least that is what I am being told. Yet I don't feel anything. I am completely numb and detached. I think perhaps this frightens me most of all—this not being able to feel and experience any emotions. Lord, how can I not feel the pain that comes with such a loss? In my more lucid moments, I can see myself as the grieving mother and step back and analyze what I should be feeling and thinking. But I'm not doing any of those "supposed to" things. I admit my grip on reality is tenuous at times. I find it simpler to distance myself from all the pain and anguish being expressed around me. I don't understand how to get myself out of this pit. I cannot even truthfully say I want to remove myself from it. For I know that when I do, I'll have to face life, and death, again. Lord, I am a coward. I do not want to live without my child. How can I go on living as half a person? For this is what I am now. I've been pierced through and my heart is bleeding. Lord, I do not even know how to pray. All I understand is that I am without recourse; there are no other available options for me now. It's you or nothing. Help me, please. Amen.

What good is God's power to you if you never receive and use it? Open the gift of power He has given you. Your life depends on it.
—STORMIE OMARTIAN IN *Lord, I Want to Be Whole*

39
Another Bug

*A*fter over an hour of waiting, Gena was about ready to pitch a fit. Just how long did the ER staff expect her to wrangle a nineteen-month-old on her lap? No question, Gena was not about to let her son crawl around on the floor. She didn't even want him touching the metal chair rests. Her son, Zach, was just itching to get down and start exploring; another bad case of middle-of-the-night attack of croup didn't hinder his inquisitive nature one iota. At first glance, even Gena might have wondered what was wrong with him. Then she, and everyone within earshot, heard the harsh, barking cough and Zach's struggle to take a deep breath. Wheezing, too—Gena could hear the raspy sound rattling between his coughs. This being the fourth time Zach had developed a croupy cough along with his chest colds, Gena should have been used to the drill. But she wasn't and never expected to become so off-handed about her child's health that even after years of experience would she ever handle respiratory problems with ease. Still, Gena tried to maintain her calm in the midst of a turbulent backdrop of sick men, women, and children.

Just when Gena thought she could not stand the strain of juggling Zach another minute, her son's name was called. Finally, thank you, Lord, Gena said to herself.

Aloud, she spoke encouragingly to Zach. "Come on, Baby, we're going to get some medicine into you and then back home to bed," Gena cooed. Inside the triage area, Gena anticipated the questions and was grateful beyond measure when the doctor started an aerosol treatment. As Zach breathed in the medicine and Gena could hear his breathing grow less strident, she relaxed. A prescription for a steroid burst and a prescription for a visiting nurse to bring out an aerosol machine encouraged Gena even more. Two hours after entering the ER's sliding doors, Gena was on her way home again with a now sleeping Zach. Once she got her son settled back into bed, Gena tried to catch some sleep. Despite her physical and emotional exhaustion, all Gena could think about was how very grateful she was to start her son on the road to recovery.

Jesus came and stood in their midst, and said to them, "Peace be with you."
—JOHN 20:19B

Dear Lord, I'm afraid. Plain and simple. I'm scared to death. I can handle the exhaustion and the strain of having too much to do in a twenty-four-hour day. But I cannot stand to see my child so sick. It frightens me, Lord. Especially at night when I'm awakened by a strangled cry or a gasp for air. I know all the right and correct steps to take to help my child recover. Still, in the midst of the struggle, I'm sometimes so panic-stricken I truly believe my heart will stop. At this moment, I feel genuine gratitude for the help we've received. This time, in this particular illness, we're on the mend. But what about next time—will it be in another week, maybe a month from now? I sometimes fear even going to sleep at night for chance of being awakened by a terrified cry. Lord, calm me now. As I attempted to soothe my child earlier on, will you work in my troubled heart and still my concerns? I do not want to live my life worrying and fretting, but I catch myself doing so all the same. Help me overcome this ingrained weakness that presses for dominance in my life. And give me the good sense to know that you love my child and me more than I can ever begin to comprehend. You gave your life for me, for us. I pray my faith will be strong and I will live each day in humble recognition of this awesome truth. Infuse me now with your holy spirit that comforts, guides, and leads. Direct my hurting heart to a place that is higher than me. Lift me up, beyond the momentary trials and troubles. And let me see your face. Amen.

A gift. A man's life. God's life. For my own.
—LISA TAWN BERGREN IN *God Encounter*

40
Rod of Correction

After considering tearing her hair out by the roots, Connie tried to come up with another, less painful, more esthetically pleasing way to work out her frustration. Connie's twenty-eight-month-old daughter, Julia, had done it again. No matter how many times Connie distracted her child away from the dog's water dish and food, Julia continued to get down on hands and knees and imitate their family pet. Ugh. Connie was distressed beyond telling. Worse yet, Julia followed Connie out of the bathroom earlier in the morning after having her teeth brushed, with two puffy cheeks full. Upon closer inspection, Connie realized with horror that Julia had stuffed into her mouth the ceramic toilet casings that covered the metal screws securing the toilet to the floor. Ack. It was enough to make Connie sick, that one. Some days Connie could laugh about Julia's inquisitive nature. And truth be told, it was comic relief to see Julia and her funny little ways, occasionally. But most days, Connie was beside herself with anxiety. I need to call a town meeting and maybe between the lot of us we can find some practical ways to corral Julia, Connie thought guiltily.

But Connie's grand solution was not to be. Instead of calling for advice from a friend, Connie spent the next two hours cleaning up the mess from spilled flour, cereals, and sugar that Julia had delightedly spilled all over Connie's living room carpeting. As Connie cleaned, she was reminded of how she used to cluck her tongue at other people's unruly kids. A deep flush of embarrassment and shame swept over Connie's face. There's no surprise why my family has given Julia the nickname of "wild child," Connie grimaced. Connie continued to sweep and scrub until the carpeting looked like new. "There," Connie said with satisfaction, "now let's get dinner ready little girl. Julia? Where is she now?" Connie said in a panic. Heading straight for the kitchen, Connie looked in dismay at the dog, whose hair was now covered in vegetable shortening. Although Julia's verbal communications weren't always so clear, it was obvious by the triumphant look on her face that she was pleased with her handiwork.

For Thou, Lord, art good, and ready to forgive,
And abundant in lovingkindness to all who call upon Thee.
—PSALM 86:5

Dear Lord, my nerves are shot. I never imagined that one small child could so control my every waking moment. I am uptight twenty-four/seven. It seems that rest will not be a guest in my home for years to come. Lord, I need something tangible, something to grasp hold of right now. Can you please help me? I remember how I looked down upon others who were struggling with their children. I judged them pretty neatly, didn't I? Put them right on a shelf between the incompetent and the miserably pathetic. I see now how very misinformed I was. How could I have been so hard-hearted and condemning? Lord, you and I both know how much effort I put into mothering my child each day, every day. It's overwhelming at times. Especially now, with my little one on the move all the time, I dare not leave her alone for a minute. I'm learning that lesson time and again. Lord, please forgive my callous attitude. I'm wondering whether you gave me such an energetic child to soften my hardened heart. It's true, isn't it? I've learned some of my toughest lessons since I gave birth to this child. Help me turn a corner in my self-righteous attitude. Give me the humility to ask for advice and assistance from others so that I might learn how to parent my child more effectively. It's clear how much I have to learn. Please provide your daily strength and infuse my weary heart with hope that in time, things will improve. Let me not give in to complacency but apply diligence to my parenting instead. I ask for your wisdom and your hand of grace as I seek to mother my child according to your precepts and principles. Amen.

Without the truth of God's holiness and the stark reality of our sin, Christ's grace is meaningless.
—RANDY ALCORN IN *The Grace and Truth Paradox*

PART FIVE

Living Outside the Box and Loving It!

Unexpected pregnancies, complicated pregnancies, adoption snags, infertility woes, languishing marriages, financial setbacks, family fights, and countless other life struggles are all part and parcel of becoming a mom. Though not all moms will face the same trials, every mother will be called upon to face down her own. At the crossroads of defeat and determination, most mothers will set their feet toward the path of most resistance. They will walk determinedly into the fire of their foes, disarm them, and emerge stronger for it. With God as their guide, these women of faith see life's challenges differently than most. Their eyes are tempered by eternity and they have the vision to look past today's pain and into tomorrow's opportunity.

41

Double Take

*A*s the current and longest lasting director for the city-run day care center, Diana, at age forty-nine, thought she had seen it all. Thinking back over her twenty-odd years of service, Diana couldn't remember another case that screamed of injustice more blatantly than the four-year-old she was cuddling at the moment. It was 1:30, story time was just about over, and little Oliver nestled himself into Diana's lap. She wondered whether he was still awake. More often than not, with the lights dimmed just so, Oliver fell asleep. Looking up at a coworker, Diana gestured toward Oliver's dark head. Her friend nodded and Diana carefully removed Oliver to the sleeping mat by her side. Diana quietly tiptoed from the playroom and swept back into her office.

Today, surely, by this afternoon, I'll get the final OK from downtown, Diana hoped. Checking with her assistant, Diana sighed. No call yet. Might as well get the rest of my reports in order while I have the time, she decided. Trying to concentrate, Diana fidgeted in her seat, sipped some coffee, and caught herself staring at the phone, all the while wondering whether she was crazy to be thinking about adopting a young child at her age. Single again after a divorce many years earlier and having raised two daughters, Diana would never have imagined that she would be so set on becoming a mother again this late in life. But she was, and if all went well, Oliver would no longer be her foster child; he would be her son legally. Diana knew it was the right decision, but that didn't stop her from fretting that something might go awry before she signed the final papers. Although Diana's love for Oliver was unconditional, she did have moments of concern that she might not possess the stamina required to raise another child. Experience, no problem. Love, no question. Energy, another matter. I suppose, Diana determined, this is just another area where faith will be an absolute requirement and not a tacked-on afterthought.

Trust in the Lord, and do good;
Dwell in the land and cultivate faithfulness.
Delight yourself in the Lord;
And He will give you the desires of your heart.
Commit your way to the Lord,
Trust also in Him, and He will do it.
—PSALM 37:3–5

Dear Lord, I'm sitting here deciding whether I should be praying for more wisdom or giving thanks for your tremendous and most generous blessing. My heart is doing flip-flops—that much is certain. One moment I'm overwhelmed by your provision. The next, I'm scared that I might not measure up to the task at hand. You know my heart's deepest desire, Lord. You alone are privy to my innermost thoughts. I do want to mother again in the realest sense. Yet there is a caution in my heart as well. Though I am doing the job already, do I have what it takes over the long haul? I'm not so young anymore. It takes me longer to get going, to keep up, and to stay the pace. Lord, even though I am doubting, I do believe this is your plan for me. So, by faith, I will believe that everything I need you will supply. From this moment on, Lord I will act on the truth, as I understand it. But I must have your insight, your wisdom, and your strong hand of encouragement to brace me as I go along. Please, meet me at my point of need, Lord. Enlarge my vision. Let me see the possibilities and the potential for good this will bring. Demonstrate to me that I am fully capable of serving you in this way. Despite my weaknesses, use me, Lord. Let my love for this child open the windows of a darkened heart. Allow me the privilege of watching a tender one blossom and grow into the person you already know him to be. Thank you, Lord, for bringing me and my tumultuous emotions full circle once again. You are my God, my provider, and my counselor. Amen.

Faced with this inevitable winter, what does nature do in autumn? It scatters the seeds that will bring new growth in the spring—and scatters them with amazing abandon.
—PARKER J. PALMER IN *Let Your Life Speak*

42
Showers of Blessing

Seated at all the undersized desks were friends and coworkers whom Amy had gotten to know over the last school season. This was her first and possibly last year teaching kindergarten. Along with bittersweet emotions, Amy was overwhelmed by the staff's generous baby shower and the gifts—it seemed to Amy that there was a small mountain of them! After opening each beautifully wrapped present, Amy said her thanks and told them she hoped they wouldn't lose touch if she decided not to return in the fall. "Come back, come back," most of the voices beckoned. "Maybe," Amy said with little conviction. Finishing up the dark chocolate cake with the luscious raspberry filling, Amy felt satiated. In every conceivable way, Amy had experienced a truly memorable afternoon. Once her friends helped her load the baby gifts into her van, Amy started toward her mother's house to pick up her daughter, Jayne.

This year was the first of many new ventures for Amy and her family. For the first time since Jayne had been born, Amy took a full-time teaching position while Jayne had been in school herself. Amy's mom had volunteered to take care of Jayne until Amy arrived each afternoon to take her home. Amy couldn't believe how smoothly the school year had gone. With her mom always at the ready to pitch in and help out, Amy never felt overstressed even with Jayne in school. Next fall would be a different story, since an unplanned pregnancy was threatening to alter Amy's plans to continue teaching. As she had on many other spring days, Amy drove toward her mother's home and contemplated their family's options. Should she continue working and have Mom watch the baby too? Did she even want to be away from her newborn? Was she up to the challenge of working full-time and mothering a six-year-old and an infant? Amy wasn't sure, and time for making the final decision was pressing in all around her. But with the bounty of that afternoon's goodness still so fresh in her memory, Amy decided that she would make no room for worry in her heart that day.

Many are the plans in a man's heart,
But the counsel of the Lord, it will stand.
—PROVERBS 19:21

Dear Lord, we never thought to be faced with such an important decision. How we planned and thought and prayed before this year came and went. Lord, we sought out advice from people we trusted, and we listened to their counsel. I believed we finally had turned a corner and had these next few years settled. And now, an unexpected pregnancy has us stymied. What should we do? All our well-laid plans are moot now. It is almost comical when I consider how much time and energy we

*invested in trying to make the wisest decision. I understand
that either choice we make now could be a good one. Perhaps
that is why it is so very difficult for us. We're just not sure what
path to take. With such wonderful and supportive loved ones
around us, we have more options than most young families. I
thank you for this precious gift of commitment and love that
we are the beneficiaries of each and every day.*

*Still, in light of these new developments, help us seek
out the wisest and best course to follow. Let not personal
ambitions or material things take precedence over making the
most prudent choice for our family. Give us great faith and
reveal to us your mind on this important matter. Bring to us
your thoughts and your ways, Lord. Help us sift through the
information and proceed with the decision you desire for us at
this time in our lives. Above all, let our coming weeks and
months never be filled with regret or what-ifs, rather let us
rejoice in the upcoming birth of a new child. Give us your
grace as we seek your will. Encourage us daily, Lord, to seek
you first and to evidence a spirit of gratefulness and thankfulness for your constancy and care toward us. Amen.*

*It's one thing to set a course and follow it. It's quite another to
find your course and follow it. . . . Whenever we serve God's
purpose, we enter into a kairos moment that is seized by God in
a way that does nothing less than change the world.*
—JAMES EMERY WHITE IN *Life-Defining Moments*

43
Little Differences

At her church's joint baby shower, Lynn sat opening yet another frilly dress for some special event yet to be realized in her young daughter's life. Lynn was overwhelmed by her church's demonstration of good wishes and good will. At this particular combination brunch–baby shower, Lynn and another woman were both the grateful recipients of a literal shower of gifts for their respective babies. The only difference between Lynn's baby and that of her friend was that Lynn's baby girl was adopted. At six months, Lynn's baby was growing by leaps and her evident South American ancestry made quite a contrast to Lynn's fair-skinned, blue-eyed, blonde-haired appearance. During one of the quieter moments after the gifts were opened and the women and girls chatted while they ate, the young niece of the woman who also shared this baby shower came up to Lynn and pointedly asked why Lynn's daughter looked so different. "Isn't she yours?" the child inquired. Lynn replied with her pat answer of late.

She'd received as many such questions as she had admiring glances over the past two months. While Lynn never minded explaining the logistics of her motherhood, she didn't appreciate the tactless comments from doomsayers who couldn't wait to tell Lynn about "foreign adoption" horror stories. Lynn didn't need to hear it and didn't want to. She was thankful that these types of remarks were infrequent. Still, always late at night, when she was especially weary, Lynn would find herself rehearsing these stories, and she would begin doubting her decision to adopt. After a time of questioning her journey to motherhood, Lynn would eventually shake herself free from these negative predictions and realize that God had orchestrated every step of this marvelous undertaking—and He would continue to do so.

Be Thou to me a rock of strength,
A stronghold to save me.
For Thou art my rock and my fortress;
For Thy name's sake Thou wilt lead me and guide me.
—PSALM 31:2B–3

Dear Lord, I am in awe of the great works you have accomplished on my behalf. You have made my dearest dream a reality. Truly, I have long desired to become a mother. Since I am on my own, adoption seemed the best choice for me. How long did I pray and entreat you before making this monumental decision? Months? Years? Lord, you know how earnestly I ached for a child of my own. And now, with my baby in my arms, I can scarcely believe it. What a tremendous blessing has been given—offered—to me. I am overwhelmed and amazed by your goodness. Lord, even now I breathe a prayer for my child. Protect her; surround her with your constancy and care. Keep her close to you always. Nurture her in your ways and let her heart of hearts learn early your immense love for her.

Just as I chose my child, so you have chosen to love us. I pray, Lord, that you will not allow me to give in to the negative comments others so carelessly utter. Help me see past their ignorance and answer them wisely. Give me your grace to be kind even when met with unkindness and lack of understanding. I want my life to be a witness of your goodness and grace to all I encounter. So I ask you to continue to work within my heart. Give me a greater portion of faith and wisdom to counter my own thoughts of insecurity and doubts. Especially minister to my soul when I am worn through after a long day's work. Lord, be my strength and support and teach me how to become the mother you desire me to be. I am your child and as such I must daily rely upon your resources to see me through the day. I'm certain that you have ordained this match between my child and I. Let me never waver or doubt that you will continue to be active in our lives, always working on our behalf as we grow into people who reflect the image of your son, Jesus. Amen.

When you face your worst fears and find God present in them, life takes on a quiet joy.
—SHEILA WALSH IN *A Love So Big*

44

Super Mom

Reaching up toward the ceiling with her cloth dampened with furniture polish, Melissa strained as she dusted her antique light fixtures. Mentally asking herself why this particular lamp always seemed to attract more dust than the others, Melissa took a final deep breath as she carefully placed the glass globe back in place. There, that's done, Melissa thought with satisfaction. Now, it's the just the two bathrooms and I'll get ready for bed. As she gathered up the cleaning supplies, Melissa almost ran her husband, Chris, into the wall. He stepped back and took note of the assorted cans and bottles Melissa held in her hands. "Could you move, please?" Melissa asked as sweetly as any woman on a mission might. "What are you doing? Do you know what time it is? Melissa, it is almost 11:00 P.M.," Chris said in exasperation. "Come to bed."

Melissa smiled and promised to hurry and finish up quickly. She'd be done before he knew it, really. Making a detour around her incredulous spouse, Melissa tore into the bathroom and cleaned like a fiend for the next ten minutes. Hardly satisfied with her efforts, she looked at her watch, knowing that Chris's patience wouldn't hold out much longer. He hated her late-night work binges. Perhaps *loathed* was more accurate. What Chris couldn't or wouldn't understand was that this was the only time of the day that Melissa could get her housework done without interruption. Sure, she could run the vacuum during the baby's nap, but to really dig in and clean with a crawling and almost walking eleven-month-old was virtually impossible. Melissa couldn't count the number of times she would just have completed a task when her son would tear into and undo it the next moment. Although Melissa realized she couldn't curtail her son's curiosity or his mess-making, she found it thoroughly satisfying to do a complete cleaning job late at night and at least go to bed with a tidy house. The only glitch in her plan was her husband.

Unless the Lord builds the house,
They labor in vain who build it;
Unless the Lord guards the city,
The watchman keeps awake in vain.
It is vain for you to rise up early,
To retire late,
To eat the bread of painful labors;
For He gives to His beloved even in his sleep.
—PSALM 127:1–2

Dear Lord, here I am again, being pulled between my desires to accomplish something I consider worthwhile without adhering to simple common sense. How I ache to get everything in order and in hand around my home. Indeed, lately I feel like every area of my life is doomed to disorder, messiness, and incompletion. I have never lived in such a state of "undoneness" before. As I attempt to see life through the perspective of eternity, I do feel comforted. I realize that these baby days will pass all too quickly. There will be a season in my life when I'll look back and long to hold my child again. Still, at this moment, I'm restless with an energy that wants to create and build and complete. Every time I undertake a project, no matter what it is, I am continually interrupted. No task gets the attention I would like to give it.

Lord, in my heart, I know that caring for my family is much more important than caring for the smallish details I am fretting over. Yet it's as though I've been forced to give up a part of me these last months, a part of me that I'm afraid I'll never regain. In truth, I don't believe that I've lost anything permanently, but I do need to accept that everything has changed. My lifestyle, my priorities, my very heart has been given over to the new life you've brought us. Lord, help me roll with these changes with good grace. Recharge me with a generous supply of your flexibility. Let me not become discouraged; rather, let me see what is truly important and worth giving my best effort toward achieving. Infuse me with your wisdom, your insight, and your love. And teach me to serve my family in ways that bring life and goodness to our family. Amen.

Much of life is spent rowing. Getting out of bed. Fixing lunches. Turning in assignments. Changing diapers. Paying bills. Routine. Regular. More struggle than strut. More wrestling than resting.
—MAX LUCADO IN *A Gentle Thunder*

45

Imitate Whom?

Sitting under the dancing shadows of the willow tree situated on the outskirts of the town park, Jenny tried to get comfortable. She and her friend Carrie decided to take advantage of the crisp fall weather and enjoy one last picnic lunch before the temperatures turned cold and before Jenny was too large with child to get up off the ground. Jenny always loved the outdoors. As she sat there drinking in the colorful foliage, she was pretty well perfectly content. That sense of quietude lasted for all of about forty-five seconds. Oh no, Jenny grimaced, not again. Before she could stop her, Jenny's best friend, Carrie, was up and running toward the swings. Let him go, Jenny had wanted to suggest. But no, Carrie would never hear of it. Even though the playground was deserted and the swings positioned too high for Carrie's little Jacob to reach, Carrie had panicked again.

Jenny watched her friend corral her son back over toward their blanket where she had laid out a sumptuous feast and, by the looks of it, half of Jacob's toy box as well. Still, Jacob wanted to run! Taking a quick look at what his mother offered in the way of entertainment, Jacob giggled, turned tail, and off he went. Without another word, Carrie left to follow—hover was more accurate—which left Jenny sitting alone, again. A part of her didn't really mind, another part of her wondered whether she'd suddenly transform into the mirror image of her friend: a walking, talking, paranoid bundle of nerves. Jenny hoped not. Carrie seemed bent on making certain Jacob never so much as experienced even a baby-sized boo-boo in his young life. Although Carrie clearly loved her little guy, from Jenny's vantage point it looked like smother-love. And Jenny knew what drove Carrie to such extremes—fear. So as Carrie tended to her son, Jenny tended to her friend—in prayer.

In whom we have boldness and confident access through faith in Him.
—EPHESIANS 3:12

Dear Lord, as I sit in quiet preparation for my own child's birth, I am reminded of the many changes motherhood brings to a family. A baby forever alters the lives of his parents. Though I understand this to be a good thing, I am also wondering how mothering will affect me personally. Will I become a person I will not recognize? What will happen to the "me" I now know? Just as you hear the cries of my heart before I even form the words, you know why I ask this. I have seen others close to me become transformed into people I scarcely recognize. They are so dramatically altered that I cannot help but feel confused. I understand that with motherhood comes added responsibility, but must it rob a woman of her very essence? Does she truly give up her person? I wonder. If these changes were positive ones, I wouldn't be concerned. But I see too much fearfulness, fretting, and worrisome talk.

Lord, I know that you want us to come to you freely with our questions and thoughts. Will you now calm my own troubled heart? I long for this baby of mine to be born. Yet I am a bit reticent that once that day arrives, I will fade away somehow. I realize that this is an unfounded fear. But I don't want to lose the faith and courage you've given me. Please help me see life continually through the lenses of your perspective. Help me walk strong and with courage. Let me not waver and be constantly second-guessing every decision I make. I ask you to surround me with your good sense and bestow generous portions of wisdom to me daily. And show me how to pass on this legacy of resilience and faith to my child. Nothing will matter more than for my little one to learn of your great love for him and to trust in your enduring faithfulness. Let me live this life with confidence in your presence and your protection. I want others to see the freedom you give your children. Let your joy radiate from within, each day, and every day. Amen.

> *Families become strong, not because they have gone to school and learned the rules, but because parents pay the price to be different . . . because they inculcate biblical truth in everyday life, conducting their relationships in the realm of wisdom, understanding, and knowledge.*
> —CHARLES R. SWINDOLL IN *Making the Weak Family Strong*

46

Setting Sail

*I*t was Wednesday evening and Patricia could see the cars heading toward the marina. She knew the drill. Within an hour, all sixty or so sailboats would be making their way out for this, their final race, of the season. Patricia could imagine the prerace tension that began building up as the crew prepared to jump into action once the gunshot rang out. Tonight would be a great sail, too. The wind was up, the sky was clear, and Patricia longed to be out there with her husband, Ian, and their friends. But as a nursing mom, Patricia did not yet dare to leave her darling baby boy, not quite eight weeks old. She would be gone for at least four hours or more, depending on the wind and weather. No, Patricia decided she'd wait until next spring to start crewing on their boat again. Still, the pangs to be out on the water were always just rippling under the surface.

Come 9:30, a very exhausted but exuberant Ian walked through the back door to greet Patricia. "We took second," he boasted happily. "Good for you," Patricia said with a guilty measure of false cheer. "And I've got even better news, this Saturday is a special race for women and I signed you up. I'll stay home and take care of the baby. You get that milk pumped or whatever it is you have to do, and don't say another word." But . . . , Patricia had wanted to say before Ian jumped up and silenced her objections with his index finger. "No excuses," Ian pressed, "the baby's healthy and fine, and you're back in shape and gnawing at the bit to sail again. Just go!" Patricia didn't know what to say. The last eight weeks had been wonderful, but she had to admit to moments when she just couldn't wait for Ian to arrive home from work just to have another adult to converse with. A whole day away? Doing what she loved best? How could she even think about declining?

The voice of the Lord is upon the waters;
The God of glory thunders,
The Lord is over many waters.
—PSALM 29:3

Dear Lord, what a blessed life you have given me. How can I express my gratitude? Mere words cannot contain the joy that is overflowing from my heart. I feel such thankfulness and contentment. What more could I ask for? I know that you are taken aback by my change of attitude. Wasn't I just complaining about how exhausted and lonely I felt? Was it me who came to you clutching at your throne for some small measure of relief from the tedium I sometimes experience? I admit it freely. I am a fickle creature. Today, I longed once again for something that could not be mine. Later on, I was offered this allusive gift and I balked at it. When will I learn to quiet my spirit and take a few moments to consider, think, and pray before I react in rashness? I know that my words frequently get me into trouble. And even today, I was tempted to reject a splendid loving gift because I was suddenly gripped with worrisome fear and insecurity.

Help me, Lord, learn how to flow with these new seasons in my life. Show me how to roll with the changes, certain of your steady hand to guide me through. I am so often unsure of my own decisions that I hold back from new opportunities. Let my heart be stilled, my soul at peace. Help me, I pray, regard each good gift as directly from your hand. And lead me to a place of complete trust. I must know that you will be with my family when I cannot be. You are the author and sustainer of all life. Still, my new mother's heart trembles when I consider leaving my young one for any time at all. I know that these heart pangs will never go away. They will be my companion and guide throughout all my days. Yet you stand with me as well. Teach me how to bring balance to my life in all areas and to see a blessing when it is offered to me. Amen.

Loving and being loved exacts a toll. But love is also a profound privilege, because you and I have the opportunity to discover what it means to be fully human.
—KAREN SCALF LINAMEN IN *Sometimes I Wake Up Grumpy . . . and Sometimes I Let Him Sleep*

47

Under Debate

Settling down around the Christmas tree, the children eagerly awaited their turn to open up the tantalizing array of gifts. Before that, the young ones had to first sit and endure another few minutes of agonizing delay while Grandma said her annual prayer and shared her love with that natural verbal acumen of hers. As the kids squirmed on the carpeting, the adults sat with eyes closed and hearts quieted. This was the time of year when the word *family* really took on special meaning. Marlene, pregnant for the first time, held this holiday especially dear to her heart as she watched her nieces and nephews exchange kindnesses and considerate gestures. Before she knew it, the gifts had been opened and gratefully received and it was time for the bounteous dinner. The women began making the last-minute preparations while the men cleaned up the remains of strewn wrapping paper and miscellaneous bows, ribbons, and tags. The kids, sequestered around the house with their new treasures, played.

As Marlene was whipping up the garlicky mashed potatoes, she overheard her two sisters-in-law discussing immunization, their potential side effects, and the like. Her ears perked. I want to hear this, Marlene thought with interest. As the two women stood discussing the pros and

151

cons of childhood immunizations, Marlene noted that these women took opposite stands on the issue. It didn't take long for Marlene to sense the tension rising in Grandma's crowded kitchen. Too much heat, in fact, for comfort. Each sister had her own litany of reasons she believed as she did. As the debate continued, Marlene felt more and more uncomfortable. I hope they don't ask me, she fretted. I'm not sure what my stance is yet. No sooner had Marlene birthed those inner concerns than both of her sisters-in-law turned toward her and asked, "How do you feel about immunization?" Marlene mumbled some incoherent statement and quickly delivered the steaming potatoes to the dinner table. When in doubt, offer a diversion and serve the food!

Salt is good; but if the salt becomes unsalty, with what will you make it salty again? Have salt in yourselves, and be at peace with one another.
—MARK 9:50

Dear Lord, remarkable isn't it? I so swiftly buckle under pressure of any kind when I sense I might be compelled to share my beliefs and opinions. Lord, how can I ever hope to be a good mother, a mother who has the inner confidence to lead my child, when I allow the smallest of confrontations to throw me into such a tizzy? Yet no part of me wants to cause dissension or disruption. I feel my gut just twist when others are combative and challenging one another. Please help me get past my own discomfort. *If I cannot speak of such insignificant matters, how will I ever summon up the courage to share the important burdens that lay upon my heart? I sometimes doubt I'll ever grow into the woman I desire to be. Even among beloved family, I am timid and lacking in confidence. Help me see past my own insecurities, and bless me with a boldness that speaks with a confidence constrained by gentle love. Help me be discerning as I enter into the conversations with others. Lead me to be sensitive and intuitive so that I might be the peacemaker between those who are struggling to understand each other. All these skills I will need as my child grows.*

Balance my desire for peaceful community with the conviction of standing for truth. Above all, I ask that you infuse me with your grace to communicate in a way that brings honor and glory to you. Let my words and even my countenance be effusive in your unconditional love. Lord, I am your daughter, teach me to meditate upon your principles and through this reflective study let my heart and mind develop and strengthen. As a mother, I will be called upon to lead each day, every day. Lord, I count upon you to do this good work within me, for on my own I am truly weak. Amen.

The faith given by God's Spirit makes self-concern laughably unnecessary. We know we're in good hands no matter what comes. And our manner of living reflects our knowledge. We relax and get on with the purpose of life on this earth—worshiping God and advancing his kingdom.
—LARRY CRABB IN *Finding God*

48
Shoptalk

*E*lisa squeezed into the padded booth of her favorite Indian restaurant. In her wake came her three sisters: older sisters, wiser, more experienced sisters—or so they thought. Elisa, being the youngest of four girls, was consistently on the receiving end of advice. From their motherly vantage point, Elisa needed and deserved all the help they could offer her. Despite Elisa's nursing degree and job as a pediatric nurse, not one of her siblings thought she knew better than they did when it came to having and raising children. In some ways, Elisa agreed. Experience frequently is the best and sometimes most brutal instructor. But Elisa had learned quite a lot about birthing babies and caring for special needs children during her six-year stint at the hospital. She wasn't nearly as concerned about making the all-important decision of what type of anesthesia to use during her delivery, if any, as were her sisters. Elisa wasn't sure yet if she would breast- or bottle-feed her baby, which caused some sleepless nights for her siblings, too. She most definitely had not decided upon names either. All these choices, and Elisa's sisters couldn't wait for her to decide, now, today, this minute. "Don't hold off, you might go into labor early," one declared. "You may be sure about breast-feeding today, but just wait a few weeks and see how much you'll wish you'd bottle-fed so your husband could take turns during the night," another warned. "No names, are you crazy? What's the problem, I have a baby book right here!"

On and on, they went. Ad infinitum. Trying to tune out her siblings' overbearing remarks, Elisa focused on the menu before her. She couldn't believe how they could carry on a conversation all around her, which was all about her, and not even realize that she wasn't an active participant. Amazing. Just when Elisa thought she knew what she was going to order, they changed tacks on her. "Don't order that! Try this. . . . It's marvelous. No, I was here just last week. . . ." Elisa gave up. Was there to be no part of her life where she was thought qualified to make a decision of her own? Rather than respond in exasperation, Elisa looked on in wonder—and suddenly she felt so very loved.

You were bought with a price; do not become slaves of men.
—1 Corinthians 7:23

Dear Lord, I have a remarkable family. They are seemingly experts on everything. Lord, I need patience—now. Help me set up appropriate boundaries with those around me. Teach me how to demonstrate courtesy and care while making it clear that the decisions I make concerning my family are mine to decide. As I learn how to tactfully disarm such strong-arm tactics designed to get me to do things as others would wish, teach me to display patience at all times. I do not wish to insult or demean anyone who cares enough to offer their heartfelt suggestions. Yet I must insist upon making my own choices as I best understand them to be. Lord, will you instruct me in this delicate matter? Help me not second-guess my decisions because of how others might react. I desire to make wise and prudent choices in every area of my life. Let me not give in to peer pressure or cave in to others when I am certain of another path to take. Demonstrate your goodness to me by providing me with the strength to say no. Be with me as I stretch myself during the next verbal confrontation. Let your wisdom and knowledge be the watchword of my every conversation and thought. Increase the measure of insight that I have and make me complete in you. Even during these uncertain and untested waters of parenthood, I pray that you will stand close beside me. Guide me through these sometimes overwhelming new ventures and place the seal of your love over my all too anxious heart. Lord, I commit my relation-ships into your hands and ask your blessing upon them, every one. May we all learn to honor each other in ways that are pleasing in your sight. Amen.

You see, peace is always possible. You can buy it at the cost of conscience.
—JAY E. ADAMS IN *How to Overcome Evil*

49

Anniversary

*O*nce a month, Claire's church sponsored a scrap-booking night, when women from within the fellowship and around the neighborhood arrived with all their scrap-booking incidentals in tow. From seven until eleven, any number of women would gather together for an informal night of talking, snacking, and creative memory-making. Claire, who was new to this mode of preserving her family's photos and other memorabilia, sat sandwiched between two "old" pros that were also young mothers like she. About an half hour earlier, Claire had made a quick stop into the neighborhood scrap-booking store and picked up her essentials for getting started. She also carried with her a large bag of photos taken of her daughter from birth to age one.

A few hours earlier still, Claire was scurrying around their home office stuffing all the pictures she could locate into a tote bag. It was then that she realized how fast the first year of her baby's life had flown. *No wonder I'm never quite sure what's around the next corner,* Claire reminisced. *Even my darling baby has gone from being completely dependent upon me to independently walking, exploring, and racing toward adolescence!* With such melancholy thoughts in her mind, Claire slumped down next to the file cabinet and took a slower, more careful study of the myriad of snapshots of her family's year. It was heartrending, Claire agonized. Already, the first year over! If the rest of my child's life goes by this fast, she'll be grown and gone before we know it. Breaking free of her reverie, Claire loaded up all she'd need for the meeting. She knew that she would learn all the basics of scrap-booking that night, but she was more interested in finding out how other moms dealt with the lightening speed with which changes transpired within the confines of their own homes and how they managed to keep up.

Behold, God is my helper;
The Lord is the sustainer of my soul.
—PSALM 54:4

Dear Lord, thank you for the many provisions you have blessed my family with. None are more treasured than our child. I am unable to express my gratitude for the joy this little one has brought into our lives. I was a pauper and didn't know it. Now I am richly blessed and highly favored. I am in awe in of the wondrous love you place within a mother's heart for her children. Nothing compares with this tenacious, persistent, and enduring bond. Every day, I awaken and give you thanks for another opportunity to share and invest into the life of this precious one. Lord, even now I could cry for joy when I consider all that being a mother has brought into my world. I never expected that I would be so changed, so altered. But I am. Former goals and plans fell by the wayside—and for good reason. I am fulfilled and challenged in new ways. Yet for all this abundance I do admit to a lack. I am sometimes filled with anxiety. I harbor a secret fear that this will pass all too quickly and my mothering days will be over. What then? I understand that I am just at the start of a long road, yet time passes so swiftly. How will I cope with the ever-increasing changes that I already see transpiring? Will I have the good grace to let go as needs be? Or will I struggle to hold onto my child with a nagging and unhealthy dependence? Lord, I know I am asking for help far in advance, but will you even now begin to prepare me to let my child grow and eventually go? Help me have your perspective on mothering. Allow me a greater understanding as I attempt to nurture my child so that she is fully prepared to live on her own. Make me a wise and competent mother, one that loves perfectly, completely, and only desires the best for my family. Give me, I pray, courage, wisdom, and insight. All these, I am sure, are absolute necessities as I develop into the woman and mother you desire me to become. Amen.

Perfect love is easy in His hands but impossible in ours, so He tells us to trust Him. Any further directive is unnecessary.
—CHRISTOPHER COPPERNOLL IN *Secrets of a Faith Well Lived*

50

Sequencing

Kelly hung up the phone and felt a pang of guilt. Wasn't this the third or perhaps fourth time in the last couple of months that she'd turned down requests for her assistance at her church? It was. Kelly had been keeping track. First, her local fellowship needed some part-time office assistance, would Kelly consider volunteering two afternoons a week? No. Next, the infant nursery was short on staff for the midweek service, might Kelly take over the coordinating? No can do. This last call was for a Sunday school teacher. Not possible. As bad as Kelly felt about saying no to each of these requests, she knew better than to overextend herself at a time like this. Kelly was the mother of two-year-old twins and was expecting their third in five months. She was sure that the next twenty weeks would fly by, and even now Kelly was struggling to keep pace with the energetic twins and their constant state of motion. Now's not the time to take on anything else, she decided.

It was a good thing that Kelly and her husband had already taken a good hard look at their bustling schedules before the twins' birth. They both decided to pare back and put their current efforts into raising their family. Kelly was hesitant at the time to begin wrapping up her other commitments, but looking back, was she ever thankful she had.

Once her twin babies were born, Kelly had more than a full-time job on her hands. Even now, with a couple of solid parenting years behind her, Kelly seldom sat down during the day. She was that busy! Not everyone would understand, but Kelly knew deep down in her heart that she was making the best choice of all: reserving her limited energy resources was the wisest path to take. *I can't be everything to everybody, but I can give my level best as I serve my children's needs while they're so young.*

For every house is built by someone, but the builder of all things is God.
—HEBREWS 3:4

Dear Lord, I want to thank you for giving me a genuine sense of peace at this time of my life. I can so easily be side-tracked by the calls for extra commitments that seem to land upon my lap. I believe that during this particular time, when my children are so very young, you would have me concentrate my efforts on raising them. You know how I sometimes long to get more involved in other activities. When the opportunities arise, I am torn inside. A part of me hungers for a fresh and different challenge than what I face as a new mom. Still, I have to be honest. My energy levels could not stand much more. I feel depleted much of the time as it is. Too many on-call night shifts, I suppose. Lord, I believe with all my heart that now is the time for me to

*nestle in and stay close to hearth and home. I want my
family to feel the security that comes from the continuity and
constancy of a mother's love. Will you help me keep my eyes
on this goal? Let me not buckle under the expectations of
others. Give me the resolve and wisdom to decline when fresh
opportunities would hinder the well-being of my family. I
love the idea of sequencing, Lord. It puts some perspective
into my heart and mind. I can still have dreams and desires.
I will see "feet" put to them in time. But right now, I am
choosing to place my focus upon those dear ones you've given
me to raise. As alluring as some new experiences might
appear, whether they are work oriented, volunteer, or simply
fun, help me temper my first reaction with caution. Give me
the sense to hold off from making instantaneous decisions. Be
my wise guide and let me learn to listen intently for your
voice in all matters. Help me keep my mind toward one purpose. In your name and for my family's sake, I pray. Amen.*

*Peace is not some abstract inner calm; it is a way of living. It is
a commitment to the Prince of Peace, who took every right he
had and laid it down in submission to the God of love.*
—SHEILA WALSH IN *A Love So Big*

51
Baby Lovers Wanted

This was it, Laura thought hopefully. She had a feeling about this one. With baby Abigail in tow, Laura hefted her diaper bag and a tote chock full of toys for Abby to play with as they visited. Laura sent up a silent prayer that everything would go well. Just as she was about to ring the doorbell, a fiftyish, clearly style-conscious woman opened the door, and Laura's heart sank. *No way will this woman want a two-year-old tearing through her home three afternoons a week.* Hoping her disappointment wasn't showing on her face, Laura smiled and introduced herself. "Please come in, Laura. This must be Abigail. Isn't she a darling?" Laura introduced her daughter more formally and then tried to match the gracious woman's poise as she lugged in her now foolishly overpacked tote through the foyer. "Sorry," Laura apologized. "I didn't know what kinds of playthings you'd have, so I brought Abby's favorites. To keep her occupied while we talked," Laura spoke in a rush. "Of course, what a good idea. Come sit down and let's get Abby settled first."

As Laura followed along, she was again beset by weariness. *Just look at this place, it's house beautiful.* Once they reached the great room, Laura decided to make the best of the situation. She looked around at the huge, carefully executed

163

décor and realized that she was breathing easier. Was that a walk-in closet filled with children's toys, books, and craft supplies? It was! A little further to the left, Laura noted the portable crib and a high chair nestled along the wall. Beyond that was a child-size table, chairs, and even a miniature drawing board and kitchen set. Laura couldn't believe her eyes. Maybe this contact would work out after all. As Laura got her daughter positioned at the table with some oversized Legos, she finally felt as ease. An hour and a half later, Laura was en route home, still thinking about the refined, widowed lady she'd had the privilege of getting to know. "It will be just perfect," Laura said to Abby. "I can hardly wait to tell your daddy that I finally found the most wonderful sitter for you while I'm at work."

Give thanks to the Lord, for He is good;
For His lovingkindness is everlasting.
—PSALM 136:1

Dear Lord, how can I express my great relief for this tremendous, eleventh hour miracle? Lord, you know how diligently we have searched for someone to help us care for our child. I have looked and looked. Many afternoons and evenings, I have followed up on leads only to be disappointed for one reason or another. How many weeks have I prayed for you to provide just the right person. And now, you have so graciously answered. Thank you! I almost cannot believe how wonderfully you have worked out this situation. I am so very grateful and comforted by the knowledge that you have been involved from the beginning. You alone orchestrated this encounter. You alone set the circumstances in motion. You alone knew the perfect match this would be. I feel as though I've been stretched to my limit, yet I understand that you use every experience to grow us up. It has been trying. Many nights I've lain awake fretting over this looming deadline. But in my heart of hearts, I believed you would faithfully direct my path. And you did. I confess that although I do not want to be parted from my child, I must be. Please help my young one adjust to this new schedule quickly. Help us both conquer our fears and lean upon you for our comfort. As ideal as this situation is, I am still feeling torn and am anxious. What-ifs are bouncing around my heart and mind. Please calm my worrisome heart, Lord. Set your seal of peace upon us all. I am confident that you will be close beside us in the coming days. Thank you again for your abundant lovingkindness. Amen.

For every situation into which each new step takes you, vacate, and let Christ occupy.
—MAJOR W. IAN THOMAS IN *Christianity: A Follower's Guide*

52

First Petition

*D*enise was what some might term a prayer warrior. She believed in laboring earnestly and often throughout the day for the needs that came to her mind. Denise would frequently awaken in the middle of the night, unable to sleep, and would take on the battles erupting between heaven and hell. It was her greatest desire and her most difficult challenge. Ever since Denise had become a mom, she'd found it more taxing than she imagined to concentrate. As the prayer team coordinator at her church, it was up to Denise to come up with fresh methods of keeping her prayer teams motivated week after week. She also headed up a yearly prayer retreat. With these two responsibilities constantly in her thoughts and pages on the calendar running short, Denise was uptight. Trying to juggle keeping up the home, working weekends, and staying current with her spouse required all the energy Denise could summon. Add a rambunctious two-and-a-half-year-old toddler to the mix, and it was nigh on impossible to remain focused on the task at hand.

On this particular afternoon, Denise's son was napping, so she debated between engaging in a brainstorming session for the church's upcoming retreat or taking much-needed time to pray. The call for prayer won out.

Settling down on the couch, Denise took her Bible in hand and read for a bit, then she laid the good book aside and tried to calm her wildly beating heart. Maybe if I assume the position, Denise thought desperately, I might get more in tune with God. On now-bended knees, with eyes shut tight, Denise began praying aloud. She needed to engage every part of her being if this were to be successful. As she petitioned God on behalf of her family, friends, and nation, Denise continued to struggle. She then began praying for some captivating idea to grasp her prayer teams' attention at their retreat. Nothing. Zip. Just when Denise was about to give up, she spied her son kneeling beside her. Glancing down toward him, she heard him whisper a single word, "Jesus." Nothing like a child to bring me back to basics, Denise thought with contrition.

Truly I say to you, unless you are converted and become like children, you shall not enter the kingdom of heaven.
—MATTHEW 18:3

Dear Lord, I am one of those women I swore I'd never become. I have allowed every other responsibility and pressure under the sun to distract me from my most vital task: prayer. I can scarcely believe how long I've allowed myself to go since I last spent time with you. Please forgive me. Please pardon my shortsightedness. Of all people, I know better! I understand how very dependent I am on you for my every breath. As a mom, I'm keenly aware of my constant need for you and your redemptive influence upon my heart and mind. Still, I've gotten so far off base with my plans, committees, and programs that I've missed you! All that I've accomplished is for naught if you're not in the center of it. You alone are the builder of my house, my life. Please draw me close again. I am living proof of how quickly one can become deceived by the urgent, beckoning voices that urge me to seek acceptance, fulfillment, and satisfaction anywhere but at your feet. Remove from my soiled heart all the dross that serves only to confuse me. Create in me a clean heart, O Lord. Renew my weary spirit with yours. And help me remember that I do not need all the bells and whistles of life to be successful—I only need you. Let me share this lesson with those I love. Allow me to serve you again, this time in childlike humility, fully dependent upon you. Amen.

Don't you want to know him so intimately that your heart touches his, until your hearts beat as one? Then you must learn to do more than pray, "Bless . . . bless . . . bless . . . give me . . . help me." You must be still enough to hear his voice.
—KAY ARTHUR IN *Christianity: A Follower's Guide*

Sources

Part One: Life Transitions

1 Jerry White, *Making Peace with Reality* (Colorado Springs, Colo.: NavPress, 2002), p. 146.

2 Mike Mason, *The Mystery of Children* (Colorado Springs, Colo.: WaterBrook Press, 2001), p. 16.

3 Max Lucado, *Traveling Light for Mothers* (Nashville, Tenn.: W Publishing Group, 2002), p. 66.

4 Calvin Miller, *Jesus Loves Me* (New York: Warner Books, 2002), p. 91.

5 David Hazard, *Reducing Stress* (Eugene, Ore.: Harvest House, 2002), p. 46.

6 Charles Stanley, *How to Handle Adversity* (Nashville, Tenn.: Nelson, 1989), p. 128.

7 Richard J. Foster, *Prayer: Finding the Heart's True Home* (San Francisco: HarperSanFrancisco, 1992), p. 56.

8 Carolyn and Craig Williford, *Faith Tango* (Colorado Springs, Colo.: WaterBrook Press, 2002), p. 39.

9 Jeannie St. John Taylor, *How to Be a Praying Mom* (Peabody, Mass.: Hendrickson, 2001), p. 55.

10 Mark D. Roberts, *Jesus Revealed* (Colorado Springs, Colo.: WaterBrook Press, 2002), p. 128.

11 Anne Graham Lotz, *Just Give Me Jesus* (Nashville, Tenn.: W Publishing Group, 2000), p. 96.

Part Two: The Littlest Big Adjustments

12 Charles R. Swindoll, *Strengthening Your Grip* (Dallas: Word, 1982), p. 207.

13 Roy Hession, *The Calvary Road* (Alresford, England: CLC Publications, 1950), p. 28.

14 John Goldingay, *Walk On* (Grand Rapids, Mich.: Baker Academic, 2002), p. 100.

15 Charles R. Swindoll, *Improving Your Serve* (Dallas: Word, 1981), p. 77.

16 John Sloan, *The Barnabas Way* (Colorado Springs, Colo.: WaterBrook Press, 2002), p. 4.

17 Carolyn and Craig Williford, *Faith Tango* (Colorado Springs, Colo.: WaterBrook Press, 2002), p. 34.

18 Karen Scalf Linamen, *Sometimes I Wake Up Grumpy . . . and Sometimes I Let Him Sleep* (Grand Rapids, Mich.: Revell, 2001), p. 16.

19 Richard J. Foster, *Celebration of Discipline* (San Francisco: HarperSanFrancisco, 1978), p. 36.

20 Randy Alcorn, *The Grace and Truth Paradox* (Sisters, Ore.: Multnomah, 2003), p. 16.

21 Mark Buchanan, *Things Unseen* (Sisters, Ore.: Multnomah, 2002), p. 127.

Part Three: Different Dreams

22 Ann Kroeker, *The Contemplative Mom* (Colorado Springs, Colo.: Shaw, 2000), p. 23.

23 Karol Ladd, *The Power of a Positive Mom* (West Monroe, La.: Howard, 2001), p. 27.

24 Jerry White, *Making Peace with Reality* (Colorado Springs, Colo.: NavPress, 2002), p. 172.

25 *God's Little Devotional Journal for Women* (Tulsa, Okla.: Honor Books, 2000), p. 262.

26 Cynthia Spell Humbert, *Deceived by Shame, Desired by God* (Colorado Springs, Colo.: NavPress, 2001), p. 103.

27 Max Lucado, *A Gentle Thunder* (Dallas: Word, 1995), p. 29.

28 Jean Lush, *Women and Stress* (Grand Rapids, Mich.: Revell, 1992), p. 221.

29 Albert Y. Hsu, *Grieving a Suicide* (Downers Grove, Ill.: InterVarsity Press, 2002), pp. 90–91.

30 Lisa Tawn Bergren, *God Encounter* (Colorado Springs, Colo.: WaterBrook Press, 2002), p. 177.

Part Four: Nurturing a Joyous Spirit

31 Jud Wilhite, *Faith That Goes the Distance* (Grand Rapids, Mich.: Baker Books, 2002), p. 88.

32 Andy Andrews, *The Traveler's Gift* (Nashville, Tenn.: Nelson, 2002), p. 109.

33 Anne Graham Lotz, *Just Give Me Jesus* (Nashville, Tenn.: W Publishing Group, 2000), p. 200.

34 Jeannie St. John Taylor, *How to Be a Praying Mom* (Peabody, Mass.: Hendrickson , 2001), p. xii.

35 Max Lucado, *A Gentle Thunder* (Dallas: Word, 1995), p. 30.

36 Richard J. Foster, *Prayer: Finding the Heart's True Home* (San Francisco: HarperSanFrancisco, 1992), p. 56.

37 Larry Crabb, *Finding God* (Grand Rapids, Mich.: Zondervan, 1993), p. 210.

38 Stormie Omartian, *Lord, I Want to Be Whole* (Nashville, Tenn.: Nelson, 2000), p. 120.

39 Lisa Tawn Bergren, *God Encounter* (Colorado Springs, Colo.: WaterBrook Press, 2002), p. 127.

40 Randy Alcorn, *The Grace and Truth Paradox* (Sisters, Ore.: Multnomah, 2003), p. 60.

Part Five: Living Outside the Box and Loving It!

41 Parker J. Palmer, *Let Your Life Speak* (San Francisco: Jossey-Bass, 2000), p. 98.

42 James Emery White, *Life-Defining Moments* (Colorado Springs, Colo.: WaterBrook Press, 2001), pp. 67–68.

43 Sheila Walsh, *A Love So Big* (Colorado Springs, Colo.: WaterBrook Press, 2002), p. 219.

44 Max Lucado, *A Gentle Thunder* (Dallas: Word, 1995), p. 30.

45 Charles R. Swindoll, *Making the Weak Family Strong* (Portland, Ore.: Multnomah, 1988), p. 57.

46 Karen Scalf Linamen, *Sometimes I Wake Up Grumpy . . . and Sometimes I Let Him Sleep* (Grand Rapids, Mich.: Revell, 2001), p. 146.

47 Larry Crabb, *Finding God* (Grand Rapids, Mich.: Zondervan, 1993), pp. 104–105.

48 Jay E. Adams, *How to Overcome Evil* (Phillipsburg, N.J.: P & R Publishing., 1977), p. 79.

49 Christopher Coppernoll, *Secrets of a Faith Well Lived* (West Monroe, La.: Howard, 2001), p. 88.

50 Sheila Walsh, *A Love So Big* (Colorado Springs, Colo.: WaterBrook Press, 2002), p. 191.

51 Major W. Ian Thomas, "Walking with God." In Pete Briscoe (ed.), *Christianity: A Follower's Guide* (Nashville, Tenn.: Broadman & Holman, 2001), p. 130.

52 Kay Arthur, "Prayer." In Pete Briscoe (ed.), *Christianity: A Follower's Guide* (Nashville, Tenn.: Broadman & Holman, 2001), p. 191.

The Author

*M*ichele Howe lives in LaSalle, Michigan, with her husband and four children, whom she has been homeschooling for thirteen years. She is a book reviewer for *Publishers Weekly, CBA Marketplace,* and *CCM Magazine.* Michele has published over seven hundred articles and reviews and is the author of several books, including *Going It Alone: Meeting the Challenges of Being a Single Mom, Pilgrim Prayers for Single Mothers, Prayers to Nourish a Woman's Heart, Prayers for Homeschool Moms, Prayers of Comfort and Strength,* and *Successful Single Moms.*

Prayers for Homeschool Moms

Michele Howe

$12.95 Hardcover

ISBN: 0-7879-6557-X

"Michele Howe presents realistic struggles and scenarios home educators can relate to all too well, then takes them by the hand and leads them to the ideal response: intimate dialogue with Jesus. Prepare to be challenged, convicted, comforted, even contemplative, as you pray the prayers of a homeschool mom."

—**Ann Kroeker**, author of *The Contemplative Mom: Restoring Rich Relationship with God in the Midst of Motherhood*

"Amazingly, Howe addresses every single issue that confronts homeschooling mothers today: each apprehension and thrill, each struggle and triumph. There is a prayer for all of us in this book."

—**Kristyn Komarnicki**, editor, *PRISM Magazine* and homeschooling mother of three boys

"Michele Howe has not left one stone unturned in this vast compilation of life stories and prayers from moms in the homeschooling community. In *Prayers for Homeschool Moms,* Mrs. Howe guides us from the surface tensions of our lives into the inner sanctum of prayer and hope, reminding us that we are never alone."

—**Susan Card**, author of *The Homeschool Journey*

This wonderful gift book provides emotional support for those who are balancing the multiple pressures of being a good mom, a good teacher, and a good wife, all from the heart of one seasoned homeschool mom to another. For the mom who is often so overwhelmed by her circumstances that she can't think straight, this book provides welcomed relief, inspiration, and hope through its "teaching" stories—stories that show the inspiring successes of other homeschoolers.

Michele Howe is a book reviewer for *Publishers Weekly, CBA Marketplace,* and *CCM Magazine.* Michele has published over 700 articles and reviews and is the author of several books including *Prayers to Nourish a Woman's Heart* and *Prayers of Comfort and Strength.* She lives with her husband and children near LaSalle, Michigan.
[Price subject to change]